Forms of Attention

Forms of Attention

Botticelli and *Hamlet*

FRANK KERMODE

The University of Chicago Press
Chicago and London

Frank Kermode (1919–2010) taught at University College
London, the University of Cambridge, Columbia University,
and Harvard University. His criticism was featured in the *London
Review of Books* and the *New York Review of Books,* and his many books
include *The Art of Telling* (1985), *The Sense of an Ending* (1967, revised
2000), *Shakespeare's Language* (2000), *The Age of Shakespeare* (2004),
The Genesis of Secrecy (2006), and *Concerning E. M. Forster* (2009).

The University of Chicago Press, Chicago 60637
Copyright © 1985 by The University of Chicago
All rights reserved. Originally published 1985.
Paperback edition 2011

This volume was first published as part of the series,
the Wellek Library Lectures at the University of
California, Irvine (Frank Lentricchia, series editor).

Printed in the United States of America

20 19 18 17 16 15 14 13 12 11   1 2 3 4 5

ISBN-13: 978-0-226-43175-8 (paper)
ISBN-10: 0-226-43175-4 (paper)

Library of Congress Cataloging-in-Publication Data

Kermode, Frank, 1919–2010.
    Forms of attention : Botticelli and Hamlet /
    Frank Kermode. — Paperback ed.
        p. cm.
    ISBN-13: 978-0-226-43175-8 (pbk. : alk. paper)
    ISBN-10: 0-226-43175-4 (pbk. : alk. paper) 1. Art criticism.
2. Canon (Art) 3. Arts. 4. Botticelli, Sandro, 1444 or 5–1510.
5. Shakespeare, William, 1564–1616. Hamlet. I. Title.
    NX640.K47 2010
    809—dc23

                        2011019444

♾ This paper meets the requirements of ANSI/NISO
Z39.48-1992 (Permanence of Paper).

CONTENTS

FOREWORD

Forms of Attention is the latest in a line of distinguished books by Frank Kermode, and it bears its predecessors' admirable qualities: extraordinary compression without loss of lucidity, accessibility to nonexperts, and theoretical currency—a state-of-the-art timeliness that has long been the trademark of Kermode's writing. Kermode's strategy is never to intervene at the first moment of avant-garde thrust, when passions are most inflamed, but to wait until the outrage seems about to be normalized, as the profession as a whole, without significant debate or reflection, echoes the new jargon and the propositions associated with it.

To the perhaps premature delight of traditional scholars, the avant-garde in critical theory has at last begun to turn its attention to an issue undeniably and explicitly historical in nature. I refer to the issue of canon formation and the fundamentally social and often nonliterary context of concerns in which that issue is embedded. This is how Kermode puts it: "By what means do we attribute value to works of art, and how do our valuations affect our ways of attending to them?"

Kermode pursues this question in three parts. In a first chapter he explores the restoration of Botticelli to the canon of great painters after a long period of neglect. His point is that the process of Botticelli's return to favor lays bare basic (and basically troubling) issues of canon formation. What he scrupulously documents and narrates here is the early role played by opinion ("ignorance"), in Swinburne and Pater especially, which helped to revive Botticelli's reputation and make it possible for the very different scholarly projects of "knowledge" carried out later by Herbert Horne and Aby Warburg to reinforce and secure—but most definitely not "establish"—Botticelli's reputation. Kermode insists that we grasp the interdependence of knowledge and opinion—a radically historical, anti-Platonic point—even as in parallel fashion we must understand the dependence of Horne's and Warburg's projects on the distinctive and time-bound cultures which produced them.

In a second chapter Kermode in effect performs the implicit theoretical point of his first chapter by reading *Hamlet* wholly in rhetorical terms, as rhetoric is now defined in the school of de Man and Derrida. This reading is a product of *our* modernity, as against the characterological and inward-directed norms of Coleridge's modern times. (For us, presumably, it's all in the game of words; for Coleridge it's what the words show us beyond the words.) The double-edged idea at work in Kermode's second chapter is that all commentary on canonical texts varies from generation to generation because it must meet different needs, and that the canonical text itself proves itself canonical by being able to withstand changing assaults of interpretation without ever seeming to be exhausted. The canonical text is "omnisignificant" (a modernist shibboleth, as far as I can tell, not a universal truth), and therefore it has "permanent value" and, what is really the same thing for Kermode, "perpetual modernity" (which could be translated as "perpetual ahistoricity"). This chapter shuttles between the theory that the text is a readerly function and product, and the traditional opposition to that theory, which insists that values (like "omnisignificance") can inhere objectively in texts.

Kermode's third chapter is an effort to disentangle this paradox (or maybe it's just a contradiction) by disentangling its enabling opposition—that of knowledge and opinion. But Kermode admits toward the end that it cannot be done. His willingness to accept the epistemological pluralism of recent critical theory and philosophy (from Feyerabend to Rorty) is balanced in his concluding pages by his insistence that the *only possible evil* of literary criticism would be its destruction of the canonical view of literature (the canonical text as a self-sufficient heterocosm), a view which traditional literary criticism has created and imposed on texts like *Hamlet*. (An interesting and wholly amusing and convincing sidelight of Kermode's argument in these pages is that Paul de Man is a thoroughly canonical thinker.) So in the end Kermode performs (on the theoretical highwire) the amazing feat of, on the one hand, going all the way with deconstruction and, on the other hand, keeping everything in its place, the canon preserved and protected, which is what the majority of the profession would want. Like all ambitious books in literary theory, *Forms of Attention* wants it both ways at once; that desire is its strength, and it will provide its focus of debate.

Frank Lentricchia

PREFACE

By what means do we attribute value to works of art, and how do our valuations affect our ways of attending to them? It is to questions of this sort that the following chapters are addressed. The treatment is largely historical; a good deal of what I say concerns the processes by which we establish the high opinion of a work or of an artist which normally precedes the most energetic efforts of criticism and interpretation—that is, the nature of the historical forces which certify some works but not others as requiring or deserving these special forms of attention.

The history of those unusual objects which vanish from the "canon," vanish, indeed, from view, but are restored after long periods of neglect, struck me as a good way to enter the discussion, and the first chapter deals with a well-known instance of such a resurrection, the nineteenth-century recovery of Botticelli, in which, roughly speaking, one sees learning come belatedly to the maintenance of values established by ignorance. Like all classical first movements, this one has a dual structure and motives which are meant to come together in the end. The second movement deals with the very different case of *Hamlet* and is, now I come to think of it, a kind of scherzo, not quite a joke but a self-consciously extravagant and fallible exercise in one kind of modern interpretation, the kind required by impregnably canonical works that nevertheless need to be talked about, and always in some new way.

I have saved for the last of the three my more general speculations on the themes of the first and second, not wishing to interfere with whatever pleasure the reader may get from the relatively uncluttered narrative. This conclusion, if I may continue what is doubtless a presumptuous musical analogy, is a set of variations on a confident ground bass by a great master, Samuel Johnson. In liberating the first lecture in particular from turgid comment I was encouraged by another magisterial dictum of Johnson's, this one from his review of Joseph Warton's *Essay on the Writings and Genius of Pope:* "The facts he mentions, though they are seldom *anecdotes* in a rigorous sense [by which he means 'things never before uttered or published'], are often such as are very little known, and such as will delight more readers than naked criticism." No one who accepts an invitation to give this particular set of lectures can altogether decline to offer some naked criticism, but it is a genre of which I daresay many other people are growing as weary and as wary as I am; so I am happy to claim Johnson's support for the subterfuge by which I have kept it, mostly at any rate, till the end.

In writing these lectures, and in subsequently enlarging them, I have as usual had assistance from Professor J. B. Trapp, director of the Warburg Institute. He may very well demur at some of the things I say about his Institute and its founder, but I am glad to say that he has not refused to accept the dedication of this book, which would have to be many times longer and a great deal more profound to give him some genuine notion of my gratitude for over thirty years of de-voted friendship. I am also indebted to his predecessor as director of the Institute, Professor Sir Ernst Gombrich, for much that I have learned or partly learned over the years and, more particularly, for a recent benefit, in the form of an agreeable and informative conversation about Aby Warburg. And of course my first chapter would have been impossible without Gombrich's biography of Warburg. Professor Ian Fletcher, another old friend, generously allowed me to read the manuscript of his not quite complete biography of Her-bert Horne—another indispensable boon. I am grateful also to Professor Donald Greene, in the manuscript of whose splendid new "Oxford Authors" *Johnson* I came upon the remark about naked criticism quoted above, as well as the longer passage to which I have made such free allusion in my final chapter.

I was honored to have Professor Wellek in my audience at Irvine—perhaps a little embarrassed, too, for if I knew a tenth as much as he does about the history of criticism and literary theory this book might be worth his attention. To Professor Murray Krieger and his colleagues at the University of California at Irvine this book owes its very existence and, if that in itself seems an inadequate expression of gratitude, let me add that I was delighted to have their invitation and remain very conscious of the kindness with which I was received and entertained at Irvine.

F. K.

1

1

Botticelli Recovered

Habent sua fata libelli, and so do paintings. The works of Botticelli were ignored for centuries; indeed it has been said, by the historian who has described with most authority the circumstances of his resurrection, that "probably no other great painter, so far, has endured so long a period of neglect" as Botticelli.[1] He died, as Michael Levey puts it, "at an awkward moment for his reputation"; but many artists have done that, and risen again much more promptly than Botticelli. He was already, it seems, sinking from his zenith in the last years of his life, probably because by comparison with Leonardo and Michelangelo he was old-fashioned, even deliberately archaistic. Vasari, upon whom continuance of fame so much depended, took an evolutionary view of the art of painting, and although his Life of Botticelli did something to preserve at least the name of the artist, he could not have thought him comparable with the very great men of the next generation, and the biography is defective and perfunctory. Botticelli's frescoes in the Sistine Chapel were overshadowed by their great neighbors, and when they were noticed at all it was mostly by way of unfavorable comparison. Fuseli was not exceptional in criticizing their "puerile ostentation."[2] The Dante illustrations could not be admired until Dante himself again came to be so, and indeed they had to wait some time even after that event. In short, the oblivion into which this painter fell soon after his death was so close to being total that one might suppose it could be dissipated only by some extraordinary development in the history of taste.

And that is what occurred. The *Primavera* and *The Birth of Venus* emerged from obscurity and were hung, in 1815, in the

1. Michael Levey, "Botticelli and Nineteenth-Century England," *Journal of the Warburg & Courtauld Institutes* 23 (1960):291–306. My opening pages draw freely on this article.

2. Ibid., 294. As late as 1887, W. P. Frith, an academician still remembered for the detailed realism of his "Derby Day," could speak of Botticelli's "bad drawing and worse painting, and such a revelling in ugliness" (*My Autobiography* [1887], 2:90 (cited in Levey, 305).

Uffizi.[3] The side walls of the Sistine Chapel began to be noticed, even by some admired. In 1836 Alexis-François Rio published *De la poésie chrétienne*, a book containing passages in praise of the Sistine frescoes; it was translated into English in 1854, and Levey thinks it induced Ruskin to look for the first time at Botticelli. (One unpredictable consequence of his doing so was the painter's important appearance in *A la recherche du temps perdu*.) Meanwhile interest in Botticelli grew faster than accurate knowledge of him, and a collection might contain "'Botticellis' by all sorts of people—but none by Botticelli."[4] Among the painters, Burne-Jones was an admirer in the early sixties. Conventional opinion was still easily shocked by the intrusion of pagan themes into Quattrocento painting; but the advocacy of Burne-Jones and, later, of Rossetti encouraged the avant-garde.

There persisted, in the sixties, a widely shared opinion which must seem surprising to us, that Botticelli limited his appeal by preferring ugly women. A solid history of painting published in that decade described these women as "coarse and altogether without beauty."[5] The first Englishman to find a way of correcting this view was Swinburne in 1868. What had hitherto been called clumsiness was now transformed into a "faint and almost painful grace," and those ugly faces took on a "somewhat lean and fleshless beauty, worn down it seems by some sickness or natural trouble."[6] Botticelli's archaisms, his unnaturally sad Madonnas, were no longer faults. Fitted into a later historical tradition, and a modern program for painting, he was on the way to joining the list of artists who had a special relevance to the modern world. Of this tradition Mario Praz was later to write much of the history in his book *The Romantic Agony*.

---

3. In 1864 the *Primavera* was moved to the Accademia; it was returned to the Uffizi in 1919.

4. Levey, 296.

5. R. N. Wornum, *Epochs of Painting* (1860), 160 (cited in Levey, 301).

6. Levey, 302.

In 1870 Walter Pater published his famous essay, later reprinted with little change in *The Renaissance* (1873).[7] Though it coincided with, and in considerable measure caused, the great vogue of Botticelli, Pater's essay is cautious enough to remember the familiar strictures. "People have begun to find out the charm of Botticelli's work," he says, and "his name, little known in the last century, is quietly becoming important." Nevertheless Botticelli is still "a secondary painter," and needs a certain amount of justification. There are Madonnas, Pater admits, who might seem "peevish-looking"—they conform "to no acknowledged type of beauty." It could even be said that there is "something in them mean and abject . . . , for the abstract lines of the faces have little nobleness . . . and the color is wan." He sees these Madonnas as detached, uninvolved in their role, like the "Madonna of the Magnificat," to whom "the high cold words" of that canticle mean little. Nor do the pagan Venuses escape this strangeness. "Botticelli's interest," says Pater, "is neither in the untempered goodness of Angelico's saints, nor the untempered evil of Orcagna's *Inferno*, but with [*sic*] men and women, in their mixed and uncertain condition, always attractive, clothed sometimes by passion with a character of loveliness and energy, but saddened perpetually by the shadow upon them of the great things from which they shrink."[8]

Yet *The Birth of Venus* reminds him of Ingres, which makes it modern; and there is also in this painter a strong Greek feeling, as of the modern world's first look back at the forms of antiquity. Moreover, the visionary quality of Botticelli significantly resembles that of Dante; and, finally, he is a true manifestation of the wonderful early Renaissance. In a sense all these claims may be resolved into one, the claim to modernity. The modern includes a new appropriation of Greek art, of Dante, of the newly valued Quattrocento. All that disparate history comes together here, which is why one can

7. Walter Pater, *The Renaissance*, text of 1893, ed. D. L. Hill (1980), 39.
8. Ibid., 43.

find in Botticelli a modern "sentiment of ineffable melancholy." His goddess of pleasure, "the depositary of a great power over the lives of men," is modern in that manner, and the Madonnas are modern in being saddened rather than pleased at what is happening to them. And so Botticelli, who depicted "the shadow of death in the grey flesh and wan flowers" in a representation of Venus, becomes a modern painter.

Released at last from his historical oubliette, he was celebrated as new, as unacademic, as having affinities with the Japanese art that was now pouring into Paris and London by the tea chest. The cult was the subject of jokes in *Punch* and in *Patience*. Cheap reproductions abounded. But although he grew popular he made on the art of the period an impression that would last into a later modernism:

> Her present image floats into the mind—
> Did Quattrocento finger fashion it,
> Hollow of cheek as if it drank the wind
> And took a mess of shadows for its meat?

Now firmly established in his new setting, Botticelli was accorded a position of eminence from which he was unlikely ever to be completely dislodged. He owed his promotion not to scholars but to artists and other persons of modern sensibility, whose ideas of history were more passionate than accurate, and whose connoisseurship was, as I have said, far from exact. At this stage exact knowledge had no part to play. Opinion, to some extent informed, required, at this modern moment, a certain kind of early Renaissance art; Botticelli, along with some contemporaries—though first among them—provided it. Enthusiasm counted for more than research, opinion for more than knowledge.

I shall now give some account of a man born about the time of the great Botticelli revival, and strongly influenced by Pater as well as by Morris. His part, therefore, was rather to reinforce and secure than to establish Botticelli's fame. Herbert Horne's is not a famous name, and he was denied even a brief entry in the British *Dictionary of National Biography*. Most of our information about his life has been assembled by Ian Fletcher, upon whose published and unpublished work I here to a considerable extent depend.[9] Born in 1864, Horne was pretty exactly the contemporary of Yeats and Arthur Symons. Like them, he studied at no university, but he had very early acquired an expert knowledge of several arts. He was also a precocious and successful collector. Soon he became a follower of Pater. At eighteen he went to study design with the architect and designer A. H. Mackmurdo, founder of the Century Guild, which was dedicated to the unification of the arts. Horne became coeditor, with Mackmurdo, of the journal called *The Century Guild Hobby Horse,* which tried to bring on this unification by publishing new poetry along with articles of artistic and antiquarian interest. Horne himself was painter, bookbinder, architect and designer, an authority on furniture and ancient musical instruments, a remarkable collector of English eighteenth-century painting, and a poet.

Horne seems to have been a rather chilly and disagreeable man—if we are to believe Arthur Symons, a surly, even sinister figure, a successful but dispassionate womanizer, and a secret homosexual. An unpublished poem, reported by Fletcher, speaks of the poet (aged about twenty) as containing in his person "the torrid and the frigid interwove," a combination reflecting his conviction that "the poetic nature is the marriage of Heaven and Hell." The line about the torrid and the frigid recurs in a half-amorous set of letters now in the library of the Warburg Institute, and Fritz Saxl took it as the key to the whole character of Horne, whom he greatly admired. From these letters we may also learn that in 1885 Horne was working at "verse, painting, designing down to drainpipes," and also painting on a settle an allegorical panel with the Tree of Knowledge and Death in a thornless rose-

9. Ian Fletcher, "Herbert Horne: The Earlier Phase," *English Miscellany* (Rome) 21 (1970):117–57. Professor Fletcher has kindly allowed me to read the not quite complete manuscript of his life of Horne.

bush. He expresses an admiration for *Parsifal,* though not for *The Ring,* the former perhaps suiting better with a certain rather vague religiosity in the poetry he was writing. With considerably more animation he professes himself keen on the music halls, wishing some rich patron would rent him a stall at the Gaiety.

This ambition will seem odd or vulgar only to people unfamiliar with the preoccupations of artists and aesthetes at this period. Horne was always serious about the arts, and very nearly supreme among them was the art of the dance. His interest in the Gaiety and in the Alhambra was by no means entirely a matter for lusty hours of leisure. Of course, one object was to pick up the dancing girls; but there is something distinctive about the aesthetics of such activities. The poet Ernest Dowson was grateful to Horne for taking the risk of publishing his poem *"Non sum qualis eram"* in *The Hobby Horse;* and he respected him as the benefactor of Lionel Johnson, and the host of the Rhymers' Club, established in January 1891; but he found him so formidable that he was uneasy about dining alone with him.[10] I mention this to provide some context for Dowson's account of a meeting with Horne and his great friend the artist Selwyn Image (Slade Professor of the History of Art at Oxford) at the back door of the Alhambra on a doubtless chilly night in January 1890. They introduced Dowson to "several trivial choryphées." "There was something grotesque," he goes on, "in the juxtaposition. Horne very erect & slim & aesthetic—and Image the most dignified man in London, a sort of cross in appearance between a secular abbé and Baudelaire, with a manner de 18me siècle—waiting in a back passage to be escort to ballet girls

10. *Letters of Ernest Dowson,* ed. Desmond Flower and Henry Maas (1967), letter of 4 March 1891 to Arthur Moore; but next day Dowson reported to the same correspondent that the dinner was a success—Horne was "charming and kind," and afterwards, at 11:30 P.M., they "strolled Alhambra-wards" but "were too late for his divinities."

~~whom they don't even~~!!! I confess, this danseuse-worship escapes me!!"[11]

But here Dowson, not his friends, is out of step. He holds himself immune to "danseuse-worship," which was, among his peers, an important cult at the time. The dance was associated with the Mass as well as with the poetic image, and from Loïe Fuller and Jane Avril to Nini Patte-en-l'air, dancers were adored; respectable clergymen as well as artists and professors waited for dancing girls in back alleys, since the ritual required it.[12] The cult was by no means unrelated to that of Botticelli's enigmatic Venuses. (I do not know whether E. H. Gombrich's conjecture that the central figure of the *Primavera*—identified by most, though not all, commentators as Venus—is "dancing with a slow halting step" had any antecedent in the nineties.)[13] At all events, a quantity of poetry was dedicated to the dance and to dancers; there were many set-pieces on Javanese and other exotic dancers, especially by Arthur Symons, and many on Salome. Out of this movement, and after great transformations, came the dances and dancers of Yeats and Eliot. Waiting in that back alley, Horne was doing nothing out of character for a nineties artist, a painter of settles, an admirer of *Parsifal,* a lover of Botticelli.

Yeats, like most people who knew him, had reservations about Horne and Image (whom Horne, facetiously no doubt, described as "the gem of this dim age"); he thought them "typical figures of transition, doing as an achievement of learning and exquisite taste what their predecessors did in careless abundance"; but he admired Horne, too, for his

11. *Letters,* 27 January 1890.

12. On some of the implications of the cult, see my "Poet and Dancer before Diagilev," *Puzzles and Epiphanies* (1961), 1–28.

13. E. H. Gombrich, "Botticelli's Mythologies," *Symbolic Images* (1972), 31–81. "Dancing with a slow halting step" is from Apuleius's description of Venus in *The Golden Ass (lente vestigio).* In Apuleius, also, she is "slightly inclining her head."

"conscious deliberate craft." Like Saxl after him, he praised the church Horne built near Marble Arch on the model of the cathedral at Pietrasanta in Tuscany (it was destroyed by bombing, like most of Horne's buildings in London). And he credited Horne with "what I must lack always, scholarship"; he was one of those, said Yeats, who helped to teach him that "violent energy, which is like a fire of straw, consumes in a few minutes the nervous vitality, and is useless in the arts."[14] Yeats is writing with the aid of hindsight, knowing of Horne's later achievements, patient and monumental; the burning of damp faggots was, as it turned out, more suited to the work Horne was born to do than any display of genius that burns itself out.

However, for the time being he went on with other tasks, painting settles, cretonnes, fenders, harpsichords; designing and binding books (he published a study of bookbinding in 1894); working as an architect; editing Jacobean plays and Herrick; collecting paintings; writing poems. When Verlaine paid his famous visit to London and Oxford it was Horne who helped Symons to look after him; he was right in the middle of contemporary poetry. His own slim volume, *Diversi Colores*, with his own typography and design, was published in 1891, the year of the Rhymers; it has forty-odd pages of poems strongly influenced by Campion, Herrick, and madrigal verse, with some fairly warm liturgical pieces and some cool love poems. On this evidence Horne was but a small poet; and Ian Fletcher makes only small claims for the verse that remains in manuscript. It is absolutely of its historical moment. Horne was a gifted minor artist at the center of his world. At his house in Fitzroy Street artists of all kinds gathered: Fletcher lists Dowson and Johnson, Sturge Moore, Yeats, Sickert, Walter Crane, Augustus John, Oscar Wilde, Arthur Symons, Arnold Dolmetsch (who built the harpsichord Horne decorated), and Roger Fry.

But this phase of his life was ending. He grew more and

14. W. B. Yeats, *Autobiography* (1953), 191.

more interested in antiquarian matters, and the files of *The Hobby Horse* show it. He became an authority on the restoration of old buildings, on book illustration, on fifteenth-century woodcuts. He added to his remarkable collection; as Fletcher remarks, the building of it with such slender resources must have required "a certain ruthlessness and detachment."[15] He quarreled with Mackmurdo; *The Hobby Horse* died; and the aesthetic phase was over. Horne grew more and more interested in Italian art. He began to spend much time in Florence, and published a scholarly article on Uccello, but his main interest was Botticelli.

In 1908 he sold a considerable part of his English collection to Edward Marsh; most of it is now in the National Gallery in London. Horne used the proceeds to buy and restore an old palazzo in Florence, acquired in 1912. On his death in 1916 he left Casa Horne to the city of Florence, with provision for its upkeep; but the endowment was spent on unsuccessful investments. The Museo Horne may still be visited, though the most important of its contents have been moved to the Uffizi Gallery.

During these years in Florence Horne applied himself with remarkable dedication to the writing of a long book on Botticelli, and a second volume on the *scuola;* until very recently this second volume was supposed never to have been written, but I am told by Professor Fletcher that it has been found in the Museo Horne. Its publication will be an event of importance. Long before he moved to Florence, Horne, as Yeats tells us, was "learned in Botticelli" and "had begun to boast that when he wrote of him there would be no literature, all would be but learning."[16] And Horne's *Alessandro Filipepi called Sandro Botticelli, Painter of Florence* (1908) might seem to justify that claim. It is regarded by modern art historians as one of the finest books ever written about a Renaissance painter; Sir John Pope-Hennessy, in his preface to the fac-

15. Fletcher, 151.
16. Yeats, 182.

simile reprint of 1980, says that it "has stood the test of time better than almost any other book about art history," and that "all subsequent Botticelli scholarship depends" on Horne's.[17] Fritz Saxl admired it for its austerity, for Horne's unweaving of the frigid from the torrid; for, says Saxl, he writes "accurately and disinterestedly in a frigid style which almost obliterates the personality of the author." To such self-discipline, to the suppression of that "torrid" streak, we owe, according to Saxl, "an unimpeachable piece of historical scholarship."[18]

It would be unreasonable to expect such a book to be very "torrid"; it is primarily concerned with fact, with correct attribution and description, with offering the world an authentic Botticelli instead of the apocryphal figure it had come so much to admire. Such work demands a proper coolness of manner. Its power derives mostly from pertinacity of research—few documents have been added to those unearthed by Horne in his tireless quest through the Florentine archives—and from an habitual accuracy of eye. And Arthur Symons remarked that when Horne "sat down to write something dry and hard came into the words."[19] Yet I cannot think the book quite as frigid as Saxl and others have found it.

17. Herbert P. Horne, *Botticelli, Painter of Florence*. With a new introduction by John Pope-Hennessy (1980), xi. Ronald Lightbown, *Sandro Botticelli: Life and Works and Complete Catalogue,* 2 vols. (1978) does not dissent from this very usual view, though he notes errors, certain and probable, and also certain disadvantages inherent in Horne's method. For instance, he probably dated the *Primavera* too early: it is a painting for a marriage chamber, made for Lorenzo di Pierfrancesco in 1482–83 (not 1477); it is, therefore, much closer in time to *The Birth of Venus* (another picture for a marriage chamber) than Horne supposed. The composition of Horne's book began as early as 1903, so he was unable to include information available only after that date; Jacques Mesnil, *Botticelli* (1938), supplements and corrects Horne from his own notes. Finally, Horne's book (of which only 240 copies were printed) is extremely long and has neither chapter divisions nor index, which certainly reduces its utility; but then he liked to think he was writing only for his own amusement.

18. Fritz Saxl, "Three Florentines," *Lectures* (1957), 331ff.

19. Fletcher, 127.

As to its design and typography it is, as one would expect of a work by Horne, an object of beauty—a book which could not have been as it is had there not been that movement in the visual arts and crafts in which Horne had been apprenticed and played a part. And the prose of the book has a sort of pedantic vivacity, a modernist archaism, that seems very much the proper style for the man; an "aesthetic" style, but qualified by a pride in accurate learning. Of course, Horne is conscious of an intention to correct the notions that had grown up with, and fed, the taste for Botticelli. He is quite hard on Pater, a main contention of whose essay "turns on the mistaken attribution to Sandro of the Palmieri altar-piece";[20] and he explains those "peevish-looking Madonnas" who conform "to no acknowledged type or obvious type of beauty" as "school-pictures . . . in which the imitators of Botticelli exaggerate his mannerisms,"[21] but which have come to be regarded as typical of the master himself. Indeed, Horne suggests that it was the resemblance between such pictures and the fashionable second-rate art of Burne-Jones that ensured their popularity. However, Pater had some excuse; Horne also explains that in 1870, when the essay appeared, "Botticelli was nominally represented at the National Gallery by three Madonnas of his school, two of them being 'Tondi': and the only genuine works by him then in the collections, passed under the names of Masaccio . . . and Filippino Lippi. . . . No wonder the attendant angels depress their heads so naively."[22] And Pater, with all his errors, wrote what Horne regards as "still the subtlest and most suggestive appreciation of Botticelli, in a personal way, which has yet been written,"[23] a work therefore intimately related to "the peculiarly English cult of Botticelli, which now [in the 1880s] became a distinctive trait of a phase of thought and taste, or of what passed for such, as odd and extravagant as any of our odd and extravagant time."[24] Pater is one of the two dedi-

20. Horne, xviii.   21. Horne, xix.   22. Horne, xix.   23. Horne, xviii.
24. Horne, xix.

catees of Horne's book. Its main purpose, he assures us, is the accumulation of information, but especially connoisseurship. We may think it in some sense also the tribute of a sardonic personality, now matured, to the affectations and enthusiasms of his formative years; a rejection of the nonsense, of the false modernity, in terms which nevertheless accept the rightness of the valuation put upon Botticelli in "our odd and extravagant time," and pay to the achievement of those years the compliment not only of the dedication to Pater, but also the greater one of a style that still acknowledges Pater. Like Yeats's, Horne's prose always remembers that master, conscious as it is of its own elegance and exactness, conscious too of its possession (proper also to the true though not the phantom Botticelli) of an *aria virile* to which Pater's could lay no claim.

Again and again we find, in this work supposed uniformly severe and scholarly, traces of Paterian taste and manner. Of the *Adoration of the Magi* Horne writes that it is the driest and most naturalistic of the works: "nowhere is Botticelli's peculiar temperament obtruded into the painting; its grave and reasonable beauty nowhere disturbed by those 'bizzarie,' that 'strangeness in the proportion,' by which such works as the 'Spring' and the 'Calumny' are distinguished."[25] More strikingly, he says of the *Primavera* that "in no picture which possesses the sentiment of beauty at all in the same degree, are there so many forms and traits so far removed from the accepted ideas of beauty. . . . In conception antique, solemn, religious; in expression modern, as it then was, Florentine, bizarre, fantastic. . . . He derives the subject matter of his picture wholly from antiquity; but of Greek or Roman sculpture, or painting, he knows little or nothing; nothing, at any rate, that can hinder or distort his vision. And so just that which chilled or destroyed Post-Raphaelite art, served only in Botticelli to quicken his vision of the world around him."[26] It seems doubtful that the insight could have found just this

25. Horne, 43. 26. Horne, 59–60.

14

expression if Pater had not come beforehand. The same may be said of Horne's account of the picture of St. Augustine in the Ognissanti, which takes up Pater's observation of Botticelli's "Dantesque" quality and gives it precision, at the same time emphasizing what Pater did not understand, the *aria virile* thought by his contemporaries to be the painter's distinctive trait: "We, at the present day, are apt to think that 'undercurrent of original sentiment' which runs through his works, and even the exaggeration of that sentiment in the many works of his school which pass under his name, as the distinguishing character of Botticelli's manner; but for the Florentines of his own day this forcible, this Dantesque air, which in the fresco of St. Augustine is first clearly shown, this *aria virile* as the Florentines themselves called it, was that which distinguished his work, from the work of his disciples and contemporaries."[27] Horne will even ask tentatively whether the secret of the painter's greatness may not be that the modern view of him—as a visionary painter—and the contemporary view, which admired his virility, might be "from their several standpoints, equally true."[28] But then the historian in Horne prevails. When restorations have reduced the original force of a painting by inserting passages that are sweeter, or "prettified," as in the "Tondo of the Magnificat," he is sure that the "misfortune . . . has contributed not a little to the extraordinary popularity of the picture."[29] When Pater finds in that painting the bizarre interest of a heretical Virgin, he may be credited with "an exquisite personal revery" but he has also done some harm to the truth.[30] Similarly, the "cadaverous" color, as Pater called it, of *The Birth of Venus* is entirely the consequence of the deterioration of the pigment.[31]

It cannot be doubted that when it came to a choice between "that modernity of sentiment and interpretation which is apt to distort our perception,"[32] and the historical fact, Horne consciously chose the latter. If Ruskin finds "strangeness and

27. Horne, 69.   28. Horne, 111.   29. Horne, 121.   30. Horne, 122.
31. Horne, 152.   32. Horne, 255.

gloom" pervasive in Botticelli's work, that is only because the *aria virile* would seem so to "a critic who, in reality, took as his criterion in all questions of painting, the refined and gentle art of the English landscape painters, and the English Pre-Raphaelites."[33]

It is interesting to watch Horne at his business of tracing the emergence, in Botticelli's manner, of the virile air. He is no mere archivist, and can command that air himself, as in his vivacious and pure-styled account of the Pazzi conspiracy to assassinate Lorenzo de' Medici in 1478. His excuse for dwelling on the event was that, after the failure of the plot, Botticelli was commissioned, in accordance with custom, to make effigies of the condemned or executed conspirators. He put them in a fresco above the door of the old Dogana, but after a more successful coup some years later they were destroyed. However, the need, in these works, to emulate the naturalism of Andrea da Castagno, who had done the like before him, gave Botticelli a new "rugged power"[34] which thenceforth showed up in his other work, first in the *St. Augustine* of 1480; the Sistine frescoes, painted before 1482, show it fully. To the expression of this conjecture Horne brings a rugged power of his own, in sharp contrast to the period prose he had left behind him.

All the same, he sees Botticelli as growing increasingly mannered and nervous as his fame was eclipsed by the new school and his line of life crossed by that of Savonarola; he reverts more and more, "not only in method, but in design and sentiment, to that tradition of Giottesque painting, from which he had so largely derived his art."[35] And here, perhaps, is another excuse for those who, during the revival, got Botticelli wrong. There is an element of truth, after all, in both Ruskin and Pater; Botticelli has his "discordant traits," his bizarrerie, his "amatorious sweetness," and his archaisms.[36] In any case they played a part in restoring to our attention

---

33. Horne, 333–34.   34. Horne, 329.   35. Horne, 308.
36. Horne, 334.

what Horne is willing to call "the supreme accomplishment of modern art."[37]

It might be reasonable, then, to characterize Horne's effort as an attempt to modify what had become the stock responses of modernity to this painter without completely denying his affinity to the relatively ignorant enthusiasts who preceded him; he wished to give to languid revery an exactness of registration, a precision that it lacked, though he did not wish altogether to disperse its achievement. If he held it at a critical distance, he also mistrusted the more pretentious minuteness of academic art history. If the aesthetes exaggerated Botticelli's sense of "loss or displacement,"[38] the professors could be nastily vainglorious: "Professor Schmarsow has informed us exactly which of the figures of the Popes [in the Sistine frescoes] were painted by Melozzo; but as I am unable to follow the arguments of the egregious Professor, not having studied in the Academy of Lagado, I must leave his conclusions undiscussed."[39]

And it is true, after all, that the professors had little or nothing to do with the revival of Botticelli. It was the work of opinion, never to be observed without its shadow, ignorance. And it was Horne, no professor—he had never studied in any academy whatsoever—who did most to reinforce opinion with knowledge, and so give to his subject, not immunity to future loss of regard, but certainly a new standing, a new attitude in the flow of time.

Aby Warburg, born in 1866, was Horne's junior by two years, and also a child of the decade that made Botticelli's revival an accomplished fact. His origins were very different; the son of a Hamburg banker, he was destined to be head of the firm, but he became a scholar instead, and a remarkable one. E. H. Gombrich's admirable "intellectual biography" of

37. Horne, 304.   38. Horne, 147.   39. Horne, 88.

Warburg[40] gives one a rather intimate view of an education that was wholly different from any that could be got, then or now, in Britain or the United States, and certainly a world away from the quite informal training of Horne. Warburg was the pupil of great men now largely forgotten—of Hermann Usener, remembered perhaps because of the phrase "momentary deity," and the championship of Ernst Cassirer; of Karl Lamprecht, Anton Springer, Carl Justi; and of that August Schmarsow who inadvertently irritated Horne.[41]

Most of Warburg's teachers assumed that the findings of modern science ought to be applied to the humanities. They were affected, one way or another, by Hegel, but also by evolutionary theory, and by the tenacity of the primitive—the manifestations, in the life of an evolved civilization, of images or of behavior that originate in some residual or atavistic layer of the individual mind or of the race, or simply of civilization. Lamprecht, whom Gombrich describes as the most influential of Warburg's masters, divided cultural history into five periods, each a further displacement of the primitive "symbolic"; and Springer was interested in the ways in which the Middle Ages and the Renaissance looked at classical antiquity. It was he who called this the study of "das Nachleben des Antike," an expression later strongly associated with Warburg.

Usener's quest for "spiritual traces of vanished times" in later cultural epochs,[42] and the many other rather similar

40. E. H. Gombrich, *Aby Warburg: An Intellectual Biography* (1970), 305. I have drawn heavily on this work in my discussion of Warburg.

41. Professor J. B. Trapp reminds me that Warburg dedicated his Botticelli study to Hubert Janitschek and Adolf Michaelis, masters important to him. One should also mention his reverence for Burchkhardt.

42. It was Usener who directed Warburg's attention to the work of Tito Vignoli, whose *Mito e scienza* (1879) proved to be of importance to the younger man. Maria Michela Sassi says that Warburg used Vignoli in a very personal way, impressed above all by Vignoli's insistence on fear as the motive behind the tendency to "animate" the unknown—a tendency that would persist into a scientific age because man "humanises and personifies images, ideas and concepts by converting them into living subjects, just as in the beginning he humanised and per-

kinds of research in the latter half of the century, may suggest a quite different variety of fin-de-siècle preoccupation than those of Horne and his circle. These scholars were concerned with the construction of theories intended to have great explanatory power. One naturally thinks of a much greater man, Freud (though Warburg himself did not care to do so) as one concerned also with the relation of the primitive, and of primitive symbols, to civilization. I shall return briefly to Freud and his relevance to these questions in my third lecture; here I mention him only as a name more familiar than the others who sought something like total historical explanations, though they looked primarily to art for their evidence of symbolic survival.

Warburg himself sketches systems in his notebooks, but the pattern of the interests underlying them is clear and persistent; he rarely allowed his theoretical speculations to escape from his notes, and he was pained by the difficulty of reconciling them with his observations. As Gombrich delicately explains, Warburg's psychological constitution was such that he must have been especially interested in the idea that history demonstrates a progress from an archaic state of terror, and that symbols or images proper to that early state may recur under civilized conditions, but purged of their original dionysiac horror.[43] This lifelong sufferer from anxiety

sonified cosmic objects and phenomena." Maria Michela Sassi, "Dalla scienza delle religioni di Usener ad Aby Warburg," in *Aspetti di Hermann Usener, filologo della religione. Seminario della Scuola Normale di Pisa . . . 1982*, a cura di G. Arrighetti [etc.], Pisa (1982).

43. "Sometimes it looks to me as if, in my role as psycho-historian, I had to diagnose the schizophrenia of Western civilisation from its images in an autobiographical reflex," wrote Warburg in relation to the Nympha (Gombrich, 303). And it is true that for him the image had a "manic" quality (he seems, both here and in speaking of his own illness, to have confused the manic-depressive with the schizophrenic). But he was not alone in attaching this sort of significance to the Nympha; Taine had done so, much more palely (see below); and so, a few years later, did Horne, who singles out, in the Sistine fresco of the Temptation, the "woman with flying draperies, who steps forward, almost in profile, with a bundle

therefore had a personal motive for studying not only the survival of antique forms, but also the evolved conditions under which they might later manifest themselves. Springer had taught him that just as the historian has always to interpret the past from his own historically limited position, so too "the object of interpretation—in the case of art—is itself a reinterpretation of some earlier source."[44] Warburg accordingly combined a perpetual interest in the recurrent transformations of ancient symbols with minute research into the social and pictorial circumstances of their reappearances. He did not forget what Lamprecht had taught him—that all artifacts are evidence; and he knew that there was nothing in the history of thought—whether of art, religion, magic, or science—that was in principle irrelevant to his inquiries.

Like most ambitious thinkers, he used other men's thoughts and systems of ideas as stimulants rather than as schemes he might or might not adopt; he was not looking for something ready-made, but for hints, for the stimulus that might give rise to a brainwave of his own. The "afterlife of antiquity" became his own subject—not in the old manner, the manner of Winckelmann, who thought of the classical influence as calm and idealizing, but instead as the memory of what had been tamed and put to human use. Images which had their origin in archaic terror, he believed, would recur in more reassuring contexts; they would then encapsulate the mentality of another epoch.

---

of oak faggots on her head. In the blithe, exuberant sense of life which animates this incomparable figure, Botticelli approaches more nearly to the spirit of Greek art than, perhaps, even Donatello himself had done" (Horne, 99). Here we may feel a curious affinity between "Decadent" and "Greek," which doubtless originates in Pater's essay. Of course it remains true that neither Taine nor Horne was obsessed with the image as Warburg was; we do not sense in what they say anything corresponding to what Gombrich calls "the subsoil of fear that underlies Warburg's fascination with the Nympha" (Gombrich, 305), its association with headhunters, maenads, and ultimately, one supposes, castration fears.

44. M. Podro, *The Critical History of Art* (1982), 157.

"God dwells in detail" was a motto of Warburg's;[45] but his observation of detail, his choice of interests, depended upon a larger need for a theory that would accumulate symbolic recurrence in changing historical conditions. After the First World War he spent six years in an asylum; on his return to work in 1924 he was still looking for a theory of transindividual memory. He found help in the doctrines of Richard Semon,[46] which concerned engrams or memory traces in the individual, and he extended this notion so that he could think of recurrent forms and symbols as engrams or traces in the memory of a culture. Artists make contact with these mnemic energies, and the history of art can be seen as a history of reinterpretations, updatings of these symbols, in the course of which they are purged of their original ecstasy and terror. In this way, he said, "humanity's holdings in suffering become the possessions of the humane."[47] He could, for example, compare Manet's *Déjeuner sur l'herbe* with the sarcophagus that, through Renaissance intermediaries, is its source, and call Manet's picture the transformation of a "phobic engram."[48]

Such ideas have a practical value quite apart from any interest they may have as theories; they provide methods of studying detail, and of choosing which details to study. In 1893 Warburg wrote his thesis on Botticelli's *Birth of Venus* and *Spring*. How did Botticelli and his patrons imagine the antique? To answer these questions calls for detailed knowl-

45. The source of this expression, much inquired after, seems now to have been found in Hermann Usener, whose method it was to seek general laws by studying a particular datum (Sassi, 86, citing D. Wuttke). Usener has several versions, none completely identical with Warburg's. Sassi shows that Dilthey has the same idea, differently expressed, and attributes it to Goethe; she is persuaded that Warburg read Dilthey. Here is another indication that Warburg singled out from several diverse threads of the German tradition the theme that had most interest for him as he constructed his own.

46. R. Semon, *The Mneme* (trans. 1921).

47. Gombrich, 250.

48. Gombrich, 241ff, 275.

edge of such matters as the relations between artists, patrons, and humanists. Warburg provided some of the answers, especially with respect to the literary sources of these paintings, and though there are many rival proposals for the programs of the works, this early study of Warburg continues to be cited and, usually, endorsed.[49]

On the face of it, nothing could less resemble the essay of Pater, or even the assured connoisseurship of Horne, than this piece of German art history. Yet Warburg certainly had, in common with Horne, a fastidious dislike for the new vulgar cult of the Quattrocento and especially of Botticelli—indeed, for all that Horne meant to exclude when he told Yeats there would be in his book on Botticelli "no literature." And perhaps they had something more positive in common.

Warburg observed in the running female figure of the *Primavera*, the breeze blowing her dress against her body, a specific classical motif—an instance of the *Nachleben* of an antique form, which also constituted a sort of emancipation from the stiff northern fashions of contemporary Florentine taste. The literary source of the poem—Ovid, as mediated by the contemporary poet Poliziano—offers a similar modern version of the antique; but the visual image has a special suggestiveness. The female figure with agitated drapery, as it sometimes occurs in late fifteenth-century art, was named by Leonardo the "Nympha," and Warburg borrowed the

49. E.g. E. Panofsky, *Renaissances and Renascences in Western Art* (1960) (Harper Torchbook, 1969), 191–200; E. Wind, *Pagan Mysteries of the Renaissance* (1958), 100–120; E. H. Gombrich, "Botticelli's Mythologies" (see n. 13); more recently R. Lightbown (see n. 17) who finds a simpler message in the "frank carnality" of the paintings than Neoplatonic or highly ethical programs account for (Lightbown, 81); and Paul Holberton, "Botticelli's *'Primavera'*: che volea s'intendesse," *Journal of the Warburg and Courtauld Institutes* 45 (1982), 202–10, argues that Warburg was in general right about sources and themes, though the lady in the central position of the picture is not Venus. Holberton agrees with Gombrich in finding an ethical intention, though for him the subject is not humanitas but the conversion of spring lust into *gentilezza*—love taming savage desire.

word.[50] Long before, Hippolyte Taine had singled out for admiration a figure in Ghirlandaio's fresco of the nativity of St. John the Baptist in Santa Maria Novella. "In the 'Nativity of the Virgin' the girl in a silk skirt, who comes in on a visit, is the plain demure young lady of good condition; in the 'Nativity of St. John' another, standing, is a mediaeval duchess; near her the servant bringing in fruits, in statuesque drapery, has the impulse, the vivacity and force of an antique nymph, the two ages and the two orders of beauty thus meeting and uniting in the simplicity of the same true sentiment."[51] But Taine goes on to admit that such pictures, though interesting, lack skill, lack action and color, belonging as they do to the dawn or first light of the Renaissance. Warburg did not feel the need to make these Vasari-inspired concessions; Ghirlandaio's Nympha interested him so much that he projected a study of the motif.

In a partly facetious correspondence of Warburg's with a friend equally interested in the Nympha, she is compared with Salome, who danced "with her death-dealing charm in front

50. Gombrich, 65.

51. Hippolyte Taine, *Italy: Florence and Venice*, trans. J. Durand (1889), 129. Taine speaks also of "dry outlines, feeble color, and irregular and ungracious figures" combined with "deep and fervid sentiment" in the painting of the period. Of the lady and the nymph in the *Nativity of St. John*, he adds: "A fresh smile rests on their lips; underneath their semi-immobility, under these remains of rigidity which imperfect painting still leaves, one can divine the latent passion of an intact spirit and a healthy body. The curiosity and refinement of ulterior ages have not reached them. Thought, with them, slumbers; they walk or look straight before them with the coolness and placidity of virginal purity; in vain will education with all its animated elegancies rival the divine uncouthness of their gravity.

"This is why I so highly prize the paintings of this age; none in Florence have I studied more. They are often deficient in skill and are always dull; they lack both action and color. It is the renaissance in its dawn, a dawn gray and somewhat cool, as in the spring when the rosy hue of the clouds begins to tinge a pale crystal sky, and when, like a flaming dart the first ray of sunshine glides over the crest of the furrows."

of the licentious tetrarch," and also with Judith. "There was," as Gombrich says, "something in the figure which struck the two students of art as the embodiment of passion"; and although Gombrich finds an explanation for this enthusiasm in the resemblances between the Nympha and the "new woman" of Warburg's own time, and the call for less restricted movement in sport and in dancing, he also affirms that "none of Warburg's published writings bears the stamp of the fin de siècle and of the fashionable Renaissance cult of those years to anything like the same degree as this abortive plan." The Nympha, whether in Botticelli or in Ghirlandaio, was an embodiment of Renaissance "paganism," an "eruption of primitive emotion through the crust of Christian self-control," or perhaps an instance of their being made "compatible," a word borrowed by Warburg from Herbert Spencer.[52]

"Have I encountered her before?" Is she a memory reaching back over "one and a half millennia"? Is the Nympha the Maenad, or a trace of that figure erupting in the art of the Quattrocento as Salome into that of the fin de siècle? Warburg is undoubtedly thinking of her in a manner for which, much later, he was to find concrete terms in Semon; she is the reinterpretation of an engram, harnessing the energy of the old image, civilizing it. She represents the way in which antique forms may be modern. By understanding Botticelli's communion with the past we are afforded an understanding of our own.

So, in his very different way, Warburg too was fascinated by the dancing Salome; for him as for Yeats, such a figure represented the survival into modernity of images perpetuated in a process of memory that transcended the individual. What marks the difference between the self-educated poet and the scholar of many seminars and libraries is partly a matter of tone, but more of the type of intellectual system that each, according to his formation, chose. Warburg's explanations

52. Gombrich, 106ff, 169.

tend to have a scientific character, as his training required; Yeats preferred magic.

Over the years Warburg built a large, interdisciplinary, and idiosyncratic library, at first housed in the Institute at Hamburg. He called it an "observation post for cultural history." Anything that had some bearing on the *Nachleben* ought to be there.[53] For the study of detail and recurrence he used large screens, on which one could arrange images and study their mnemic interrelations; these screens he would carry across Europe in trains, a rich man's instruments for the study of cultural memory traces, a service to Mnemosyne, whose name was to give him the title of his last projected book. On such screens one might see the relation between Judith and an ancient female headhunter and also the sublimated image of a girl carrying a basket of fruit; she might be the Nympha as the Hora of Autumn, or Rachel at the well, in Botticelli's Vatican fresco. More playfully, perhaps, one connects a maenad with a female golfer. Gombrich illustrates the Nympha screen: a tondo by Filippo Lippi, examples of the classical origin of blown veils, an early Christian ivory, a photograph of an Italian peasant with a head basket, debased nymphs on travel posters. Warburg called the screen *Das Märchen vom Fraulein Schnellbring*—another jest, but he also associated her with manic states, in himself and in cultural history.[54]

It is easy to see that his work was both facilitated and constrained by his own psychology, and he pursued it passionately without ever fully justifying his method. Gombrich re-

53. Sassi, 90, records the "stupefaction" of Ernst Cassirer when he went to the Institute in Hamburg in 1920 and saw that Warburg, then still very little known, had brought together in the library—as if for him personally—all that material, placing books on magic beside those on astrology and folklore, associating art, literature, and philosophy in the manner most suitable for his grasping the relations between the various "symbolic forms."

54. Gombrich, 297–302.

marks that it is impossible to tell where "the metaphor of survival ends and where a belief in the independent life of these entities [the archaic symbols] begins."[55] But perhaps it is never simple to distinguish between the systematic expression of beliefs, and needs or drives more obscure, for which such systems may serve as metaphors.

The study of the *Nachleben* has taken new forms, though they are recognizably in the Warburg tradition, and testify to the continuance of his passion for detail, his cult of Mnemosyne. He was himself unusually aware that forgetting and mistaking were important parts of the action of memory. He pointed to the errors of the Florentine *camerata*, which sought to revive ancient music, misunderstood it, and so helped to make possible modern opera.[56] He knew that the pagan deities, which had survived in almost unrecognizable forms until restored to their old splendor and granted their original attributes in the Renaissance, were nevertheless not what they had been; their potency was altered, their place and play in the minds of later men was different; even an antique statue could not be looked on with ancient eyes. What is made of such things, he said, "depends upon the subjective make-up of the late-born rather than on the objective character of the classical heritage. . . . Every age has the renaissance it deserves."[57] He was none the less anxious to correct the misunderstandings of earlier scholars as to the true historical character of the Italian Renaissance, hoping no doubt that his own age deserved the truth.

His Institute, smuggled out of Nazi Germany, received in London, and now firmly established in Bloomsbury, had a history he could not possibly have foreseen, and work is done there that he could not have predicted. The language spoken in the corridors is no longer for the most part German, and the present director is the first to have English as his native language. But the library remains recognizably Warburg's, designed, as they say, to lead you not to the book you're looking for but to the one you need. The photographic collection still services Warburgian screens though I don't suppose the images thereon are thought of as engrams, and the familiar Warburg lecturing style still requires two projectors for the comparison of images. Over the door is written, in Greek characters, MNEMOSYNE.

"Of the general ideas to which I attach so much importance," wrote Warburg, "it will perhaps be said or thought one day that there was at least one thing to be said for these erroneous schematisms, that they excited him to churn up individual facts which had been unknown before."[58] About his having done much useful churning up of facts there is absolutely no argument; but much more than fact survives. It is perfectly possible to see in, for example, Panofsky's work on renaissance and renascence, and on the interplay of history and interpretation—on the *Nachleben,* as it were, of theories concerning the *Nachleben*—or in Gombrich's very different interest in memory and symbolism and his eye for the significant detail, transformations of recognizably Warburgian themes and precepts. When Sir Ernst recently told the American Academy of Arts and Science that the humanities were the memory of culture, he was, perhaps with deliberation, saying what his predecessor might have said on such an occasion. As we have seen, the interpretation of the Botticelli Venuses continues with many variations; but however they differ, they are all conscious of the tradition in which they have their place, and of Warburg's importance in its constitution. It is indeed inconceivable that such interpretation should ever come to a stop, or that it should not contain error, or that the mood of a later generation's understanding should exactly imitate that of its predecessors. If we have systems they will not be the systems of those predecessors. As Michael Podro says at the end of his study of the German art-historical tradition, "no system, no systematic viewpoint could be regarded as identical with our thought and viewpoint. To

58. Gombrich, 305.

make such an identification would be incompatible with the mind retaining its freedom."[59] And yet there *is* continuity, there *is* a tradition.

Here then are two scholars, one of them bringing to the Quattrocento and especially to Botticelli all that he had learned from a largely German tradition of scholarship, the other discovering his admiration for the painter and his interest in Florentine history as he worked and played among the artists, poets, and dancers of fin-de-siècle London. Florence was the source and focus of their wholly independent inquiries; had there been no ignorant vogue of Botticelli it is hard to imagine that the two could ever have met or, indeed, wanted to meet. But meet they did, and in Florence. Academic and amateur, each respected the other's scholarship, and Horne speaks of Warburg in tones very different from those in which he referred to that other German Quattrocento specialist, Schmarsow. They became friends, and when Warburg was not in Florence they corresponded. Then war divided them; but when Horne was dying in Florence in 1916 Warburg went to see him, citizen though he was of an enemy nation, and Warburg a patriotic German.

So these two scholarly lives improbably came together; but Horne's *Nachleben* has diverged very widely from Warburg's. Like its founder, the Museo Horne is little known, while Warburg's Institute, founded in Hamburg, flourishes transformed in Horne's native city, indeed in Bloomsbury, the scene of so much of Horne's activity; not a city or a quarter in which Warburg would ever have imagined it. Horne was not rich, and in any case would not have wanted to establish an academy; like his friend Berenson, he deeply distrusted German scholarship. All the two—Warburg and Horne—had in common were a belief that truth lived in detail, and a passion for the Quattrocento and especially for Botticelli—a painter of whom, had they been born a century earlier, they

59. M. Podro, *The Critical Historians of Art* (1982), 214.

might never have heard or, if born half a century earlier, might not have considered worth more than a glance or a passing thought.

That they were both affected by a movement of taste over which they had no control, I hope I have shown. Horne, for all his strictures, polite or otherwise, on Pater, Ruskin, and the art of his youth, could not escape altogether from what he called "literature"; his Botticelli may have the *aria virile* attributed to the painter by his tough Florentine contemporaries, but he is also the visionary, melancholy and sometimes bizarre, whom Pater saw, or thought he saw. Warburg, though so much more remote from avant-garde myth and fashion, could not altogether avoid infection by the Romantic Agony, nor by the association of the dancer with the secret perfections of art that so dominated the aesthetic thought of his younger years. He too sought to be objective; but there is an important difference in the manner of his objectivity and Horne's. Warburg considered the significance of detail (of the Nymph's drapery or her flowers) against a background of cultural history that had no discernible limits; he needed, in principle, all knowledge to understand the cultural memory. Its archaic recurrences in an evolving civilization must be studied in science, magic, and religion, as well as in art. Behind him stood those powerful, schematizing professors. Horne's confidence in his own eye and his own mind must have seemed extraordinary to Warburg. He was not at all aware, so far as one can tell, of any difficulty to be faced in seeing his subject with a time-transcending eye. He has no interest in method; the archives are enough. And if we set aside, as of course we should not, the peculiar chill distinction of his prose, and his admirable conduct of a complicated narrative, we might think of his book as a work to be subsumed by other books, as the archives yield more information (though in fact they have yielded little; it does not take Pope-Hennessy long, in his preface to the new edition, to list the points on which Horne has been superseded or shown to have been wrong). There is behind Horne's work no such theory of art and culture as Warburg wanted, no symbolism, no doctrine of memory, whether literally or metaphorically intended. There is no myth to discount, except perhaps that of the independence of empirical observation from theory.

Botticelli became canonical not through scholarly effort but by chance, or rather by opinion. He was thereafter available to these two scholars, who accepted while wishing to inform that opinion, who were touched by the taste of their own time, but who brought to the task of converting opinion into knowledge methods and temperaments very diverse. In Horne's masterpiece there is little to discard, which may represent a failure of intellectual ambition. From Warburg there is a heritage not only of findings but of methods and attitudes; and these, as he knew, would need to be modified or even discarded, either because of discoverable faults or because it is in the nature of such things to be rejected, because new work may need new thinking about the whole huge subject, even if what must be seen anew is minute. What is left is a deposit of know-how, hints as to possible procedures, ways of deciding the true nature of problems. The relegation of "theory" into partial oblivion may sometimes be slowed, inasmuch as powerful institutions can, up to a point, slow temporal change. But usually it is quick, and its use is primarily the consolidation of some work of art, perhaps only in explanation of why it *is* canonical, why it should call for repeated attempts at interpretation. There are what Donne grandly called "unconcerning things, matters of fact," and Horne discovered a great many of them, as perhaps he did about the uncanonical members of the *scuola*. But they will not maintain the life of a work of art from one generation to another. Only interpretation can do that, and it may be as prone to error as the ignorant opinion that first brought Botticelli into question among the learned.

But I am now generalizing vaguely about issues which are the proper subject of my third chapter. And before I can return to them, I have to look at a quite different case: that of a work so immovably established as canonical that it raises issues entirely different from those presented by the nine-teenth-century reception of Botticelli, and the consolidations afforded by archival research and art-historical theory. If one allows the assumption that something new ought regularly to be said, how is one to say something new, and not manifestly absurd, about *Hamlet*?

2

2

Cornelius and Voltemand

DOUBLES IN *HAMLET*

We have seen Botticelli rescued from oblivion, or something like it, and at least begun to consider how it was done, and what the implications are of its having been done thus. I now turn to the almost opposite case of *Hamlet*—a work that from the first appears to have enjoyed great celebrity, and which, it is safe to say, could only be deprived of our esteem by some almost unimaginable revolution in taste.

It is true that attempts have been made to dislodge *Hamlet* from its eminent position in the secular canon. Voltaire, in the course of his long campaign against Shakespeare, said the play was without rule, *une pièce grossière et barbare,* that would in France be suitable only for peasants.[1] Obviously he took a wholly different view of the qualities honest men should venerate in art; and his view did not prevail. Had it done so, we should all be living in a completely different world, for so great a change in our ways of estimating value could not occur without an upheaval of even greater extent in culture and society. Tolstoy, who chose *King Lear* as his special target, was aware of the extent of his task, for he was attacking not only a grossly overvalued play but the corruption of a society which upheld that valuation, to the detriment of its members. Of *Hamlet,* he complained that the hero had no character at all, despite the encomia of the learned. Shakespeare idolatry was the creation, he believed, of the German Enlightenment, which he regarded as disastrously irreligious. To succeed in his assault he would have had to succeed with his own new religion, and contrive a future society the happier for not having Shakespeare or, for that matter, *Anna Karenina.* Another famous attack, Rymer's on *Othello,* was based on the critic's conviction that he knew exactly what a tragedy ought to be, as to both its form and its ethical purpose. Time demonstrated that he did not; that *Othello* was capable, as on the

References to *Hamlet* are to the Arden edition, ed. H. Jenkins (1981). For all other works of Shakespeare I refer to *The Riverside Shakespeare,* ed. G. B. Evans (1974).

1. See Paul S. Conklin, *A History of Hamlet Criticism: 1601–1821* (1957).

evidence of Gabriel Harvey *Hamlet* had been from the beginning, of pleasing the wiser sort.

That it did so by offering them the possibility of saying the
most extraordinarily different things about it one can see from
the history of *Hamlet* criticism. Conklin supplies the evidence
for masculine and primitive, humane, gay and solemn, pensive
and genteel, weighty and wild, cautious, coarse, heroic, weak,
supersubtle, and delaying Hamlets. In 1778 the prince was
naturalized German, and Goethe produced not only the "fla-
grant impressionism" of his critique in *Wilhelm Meister* but
some observations, possibly in the end more influential, on the
partly occulted integrity and unity of the whole play, as distinct from the character.

Behind Goethe, and behind Friedrich Schlegel and Coleridge also, one may discern the loom of philosophical meditations proper to themselves and their time rather than to
Shakespeare and his, and it is the mark of a powerful critic
that one can do this. Such a critic will alter the current of
traditional commentary by force, and that force is the product
of a mind itself alienated from the commonplace by operations on a broader scale than normal criticism can or need
attempt. The effect of such work is always to make the work
under consideration look different, to alter its internal bal-
ances, to attend to what had been thought marginal as if it
must be brought closer to the center, even at the cost of
losing what had hitherto seemed manifestly central.

Since we have no experience of a venerable text that en-
sures its own perpetuity, we may reasonably say that the medium in which it survives is commentary. All commentary on
such texts varies from one generation to the next because it
meets different needs; the need to go on talking is paramount,
the need to do it rather differently is equally urgent, and not
less so because the provision of commentary is a duty that has
now devolved upon a particular profession, a profession
which, at any rate until recently, has tended to judge the
achievement of its members by their ability to say something
new about canonical texts without defacing them. Respect for

the plain sense is a very ancient restriction on wild interpretation, but the hermeneutical guidelines or *middot* of the early
rabbis were not merely restrictive; they gave one useful tips
about how to achieve new interpretations. If we were now to
construct our own *middot,* one of them might well be: what
has been thought marginal may belong more properly in the
center. Fifty years ago, "character" was ousted from its central position (though not, I think, among ordinary readers and
playgoers and, of course, not among actors), and there was a
great deal of work on imagery and on the plays as poetry. It
does not matter that much of this work is forgotten, or that
we hear less about the Freudian Hamlet than the Lacanian—
if, indeed, we now hear much of that. There must be new
appraisals, and they will be possible only so long as new relations, new adjustments of center and margin, are perceived in
the play and given licit expression in commentary.

It may be that to be conscious of this state of affairs is to
recognize an element of play in all commentary—as, indeed,
the rabbis did, without for a moment supposing that what they
were doing wasn't serious; the most serious thing in the
world, in fact. I mention this because in what follows I am
conscious that a sort of game is being played. *Hamlet* is not
the Torah, but it can still permit or be patient of attentions
that are, in a very restricted and "ludic" sense, quasi-
rabbinical.

I begin by reflecting, which seems the right word, on shadows and shows, on substance and its images, and on mirrors,
in some earlier works of Shakespeare. Lucrece is troubled by
shadows, and hopes Tarquin might be, in his turn. Hecuba in
the Troy tapestry is a "sad shadow" or reflection of Lucrece,
a silent image of herself to which she can give speech. This is
a deceptive doubling, for Lucrece's resemblance to Hecuba
lies only in the fact that the rape was comparable to the fall of
Troy, Hecuba's city treacherously penetrated. But Hecuba is
an image of the ruin.

In Sonnet 37 the son is called the father's shadow, but is

active when his father cannot be, and so has more substance than the father. The beloved, as seen in a dream, may be only a shadow; but his "shadow shadows doth make bright" (43); and this collision of shadows, which produces a bright image, promotes in the next line a collision of "forms"—"How would thy shadow's form form happy show"—where the noun doubles the verb and produces a show, an appearance, a display, that is here, though not everywhere, "happy." There is no shadow without a substance, no show without a form that forms it. A beauty such as that of the youth must have many shadows, types of which it is the fulfilling antitype. "What is your substance, whereof are you made / That millions of strange shadows on you tend?" (53). Those types may be Helen, or Adonis, or perhaps a rose ("Why should poor beauty indirectly seek / Roses of shadow, since his rose is true?" [67]), that is: actual roses are insubstantial, just phenomenal surrogates of the noumenal rose, the youth.

The relation between the substance and its representation as shadow or reflection or show is always a difficult one, and—as I have hinted—may tempt the poet or his critic into theological and philosophical complexities. The word "show" itself is very slippery. Does the "sweet virtue" of the youth answer his "show" or is his beauty like that of Eve's apple, which was only an apparent good (93)? "They that have power to hurt and will do none, / That do not do the thing they most do show" (94) is a celebrated difficulty, but at least the contrast between what appears and what is actually done is clear. And even in the Sonnets the world, which is a stage, is also a show ("this huge stage presenteth nought but shows" [15]). Shadow and substance, show and reality, are paired opposites. Together they express paradox, impossibility, *concordia discors* or *discordia concors,* something that, perhaps fascinatingly, comes between a lover and his desire: "the master-mistress of my passion" (20). Sex is an emblem of these conjoined disjuncts, as we shall see.

In the theater, itself the double of the world, its own Globe, Shakespeare early showed an interest in doubles. The comic tradition offered him twins, and in *Comedy of Errors* he doubled Plautus's doubles. *Two Gentlemen of Verona* has a pair of lovers, one faithful and the other not, together with a great deal of talk about shadow and substance. The treacherous Proteus asks Silvia, his friend's beloved, for her picture:

> For since the substance of your perfect self
> Is else devoted, I am but a shadow;
> And to your shadow will I make true love.

Julia, his own girl, happens to be eavesdropping on this scene, and remarks, aside, "If 'twere a substance you would sure deceive it, / And make it but a shadow as I am"; and Silvia then answers Proteus: "I am very loath to be your idol, sir, / But since your falsehood shall become you well / To worship shadows and adore false shapes . . . ," she will let him have her picture (4.2.123ff). This beautiful little scene is a lot more complicated than it looks. Proteus rather drags in the shadow-substance opposition to say that Silvia's being sworn to Valentine reduces him to a condition in which he is fit only to love an image, not a substance. Julia remarks that if that shadow-image were a substance, the perfidy of Proteus would soon reduce it to a shadow anyway; this is what he has done to her, and she is in another sense a shadow, being in disguise as a boy, and so a shadow or false show of her substantial self. Silvia, perhaps noticing the word "devoted," reflects that a shadow is an image and an image is an idol, a graven image, so that it is appropriate for the false Proteus to bow down before something equally false, like a false image of the true God. Of course everybody concerned is playing a part in a show, and indeed the two females are shows in another sense, for Silvia is a boy pretending to be a girl, a master-mistress, and Julia a boy pretending to be a girl pretending to be a boy.

Since all this doubling is very theatrical, we need not be surprised that it is not confined to comedy. *Titus Andronicus* shadows the Ovidian story of Tereus. Ovid's rapist is replaced in Shakespeare by two rapists, Demetrius and Chiron.

The torment of Lavinia is double that of Ovid's Philomela, who had her tongue cut out to prevent her revealing the identity of her assailant; Lavinia also has her hands cut off to prevent her writing the names, writing being a double or shadow of speech, available to the shadow Lavinia but not to the substantial, oral Philomela. Thus the play invites us to emulate the crazy hero, and take "false shadows for true substances" (3.2.80). The figure is used repeatedly in the *Henry VI* plays, sometimes not very persuasively (Talbot as shadow of his substance, the troops, *I Henry VI* 3.5.45), sometimes perfunctorily, as when King Charles of France, reduced to the status of viceroy, will be but a shadow of his former self (*I Henry VI,* 5.4.133ff.) or when (*II Henry VI,* 1.1.13–14) an ambassador is the shadow of his king; but sometimes with more of the usual complexity, as when Clarence and Warwick in *III Henry VI* (4.6.) become the double shadow of King Henry, with the suggestion that, although the king must be the substance, it is the shadows who do the real work.

More or less simple variations on the theme crop up in other history plays (see, for instance, *King John* 2.1.496ff), but the only occurrence I need to discuss here is the difficult one in *Richard II.* Bushy is consoling the Queen after the departure of Richard (2.2.144ff):

> Each substance of a grief hath twenty shadows,
> Which show like grief itself, but is not so;
> For sorrow's eyes, glazed with blinding tears,
> Divides one thing entire to many objects,
> Like perspectives, which rightly gaz'd upon
> Show nothing but confusion; ey'd awry
> Distinguish form; so your sweet Majesty
> Looking awry upon your lord's departure,
> Find shapes of grief, more than himself, to wail,
> Which, look'd on as it is, is nought but shadows
> Of what it is not.

Bushy's consolatory conceit is based on the optical trick called anamorphosis, which interested some sixteenth-century painters; a famous example is Holbein's picture *The French Ambassadors* (1533), in which between the feet of the two men there is an elliptical shape, without form when looked at from the front but, if eyed awry, representing a skull, a memento mori. Sometimes these formless shapes could be interpreted only by the use of prisms and lenses; over a century after Holbein, memorial portraits of Charles I were thus kept secret. Ordinary people were familiar with anamorphosis in the form of "perspectives," double pictures, usually portraits, painted on the same ground in such a way that you saw one of them if you looked at the painting from one side and the other if you moved to the other side; from the front you saw only confusion. Shakespeare mentions these trick pictures more than once; see, for example, *Antony and Cleopatra* (2.5.116–117), "Though he be painted one way like a Gorgon / The other way's a Mars." The most important use of the idea, as we shall see, is in *Twelfth Night*.

Bushy, then, is saying that the tearful eyes of the Queen are multiplying one substantial grief into many shadowy griefs, griefs of show. But, having launched thus into a figure from optics, he develops it: the Queen is like somebody looking at a perspective from the front ("rightly") and seeing nothing but a confusion of shapes or shadows, whereas from the side, eyeing it awry, she would see there was only one substantial figure, one grief. Unfortunately Bushy gets into a muddle, and says the Queen has been eyeing the object awry, and the conceit doesn't work out neatly, though the confusion seems not entirely inappropriate.

In the Deposition scene Richard sends for a looking-glass, and when he gets it, talks for a while like a sonnet; after studying his reflection he smashes the mirror: "How soon my sorrow hath destroy'd my face," he says, and Bolingbroke tells him "The shadow of your sorrow hath destroy'd / The shadow of your face." He knows the image in the glass was a shadow, and thinks he knows that the emotion, whether of rage or petulance, that caused Richard to break the mirror was the shadow thrown from a substantial sorrow, a false outward show of it. Richard takes some satisfaction in what Bolingbroke suggests, and glosses that suggestion in a way that makes it rather more sympathetic than was perhaps intended:

> 'Tis very true, my grief lies all within,
> And these external manners of laments
> Are merely shadows to the unseen grief
> That swells with silence in the tortur'd soul.
> There lies the substance . . . (4.1.291ff.)

It is not always easy, when kings are concerned, to distinguish shadow and substance. Of the King's two bodies, which is substance and which shadow? Stripped of his "additions"—"unking'd," in Richard's word—Lear asks who can tell him what he is, and only the Fool can: "Lear's shadow" (1.4.230–31). The robes of kings and magistrates, their additions, make a brave show, but they are the substance of their offices and powers. The king's two bodies, then, are substance to each other's shadow; and they are in a hermaphroditic union only death can end.

In theaters, mirrors of the world, but also elsewhere, as when the Lord Mayor sends his Show through London streets, what is put on is called a show. It might be simple ("some show to welcome us to town," *Taming of the Shrew* 1.1.47) or spectacular, like the Show of Kings in *Macbeth,* or the sort of parade you find in history plays, meant to please "Those that come to see / Only a show or two" (*Henry VIII,* Prologue). Or it might be a dumbshow. Whatever it is, the purpose of it is to demonstrate and display, to give outward expression to sentiments or propositions which may or may not correspond to inward truth. The theater is a scene of deception as well as of reflection, and actors are imperfect shadows in the show. Macbeth wants to put out the candle that throws the shadow of life, a walking shadow; the notion at once makes him think of an actor strutting and fretting in a show, and helping to tell an idiot tale, signifying nothing. Shakespeare seems not to have thought much of the profession; an actor was what Donne called "an ordinary nothing," a shadow, the mere show of a substance. To Coriolanus all acting is hypocrisy, false show.

The theater offered more doublings, all related to substance/shadow, stage and world. I have mentioned the twins of ancient comic tradition; but girl and boy twins were especially interesting as a kind of divided hermaphrodite. The simultaneous appearance of Viola and Sebastian at the end of *Twelfth Night* is thus greeted by Orsino: "One face, one voice, one habit and two persons! / A natural perspective that is and is not!" (5.1.216–17). Bushy's optics are here imposed on Plato's hermaphrodite, and the metaphysical affirmation of the play (" 'That that is is' . . . for what is 'that' but 'that,' and 'is' but 'is'?" [4.2.19ff]) is represented in an emblem that is also an optical illusion. Viola herself, the boy who is not boy but girl, not girl but boy (I am not that I play," 1.5.184; "I am not what I am," 3.2.141), then finally, wearing truthful woman's weeds, to be girl though only in show, appeals to the taffeta taste of the period, to a sort of delight in erotic indeterminacies, fed by the theater and its boy players, deplored by the preachers who cited the definiteness of the Law against these antinomian erosions of the borderline between one thing and another.[2] It is Feste as Sir Thopas who declares that that that is is, and the boy Viola who confutes him by being and not being at once, and by standing within the perspective with her twin brother, identical but distinct images.

Among Shakespeare's twins, by the way, we should probably count *A Midsummer Night's Dream* and *Romeo and Juliet*, comic and tragic variants of the Pyramus and Thisbe story. Since that story, reduced to farce, is also the theme of Bottom's play, the comedy is itself double, and antithetical, and its language reminds us that it is. "Methinks I see these things with parted eye," says Demetrius, "When everything seems double." "So methinks," replies Helena, "And I have found Demetrius like a jewel, / Mine own and not mine own"

2. See L. Jardine, *Still Harping on Daughters* (1983), chap. 1.

(4.1.189ff). Earlier she had told Hermia that as girls they "grew together / Like to a double cherry, seeming parted, / But yet an union in partition" (3.2.208ff), which is a highly characteristic Shakespearian state of affairs. The fairy kingdom doubles Athens, and the play itself is a shadow of the world's substance. As to the actors, "the best in this kind are but shadows." What is, and what is shown, are also an important pair in *Troilus and Cressida,* a play about truth and its shadow, opinion, in which heroes discover that glory is what you see only in the reflection of a steel gate, or of others' eyes, or hear in the reverberation of an arch, magnifying and distorting the shout of pride (3.3.115ff). Cressida, to the parted eye of Troilus, is at last split in two, a woman and a man's antithetical opinion of her (5.2.146). Even in *Julius Caesar,* where so much is done to ensure that one man should be but a man (*Antony and Cleopatra,* 2.6.19), there are two Cinnas, the politician and his shadow, the poet, twinning a hint in Plutarch with a hint in Suetonius, the mob, tyrannical as Caligula, killing the shadow because the substance is not at hand,[3] as the conspirators kill the mortal Caesar rather than his imperial substance, which is transmitted to the chilly but divine Augustus. *King Lear* twins follies, the King's and the Fool's, the King's and Poor Tom's, for Poor Tom is that mortal body, Lear's shadow. Edmund and Edgar are false, Regan and Goneril true doubles, like the boy who buttered the horse's hay and his sister who knapped the eels on the head. *Antony and Cleopatra* gives us Rome and Egypt as in a perspective, one rock hard, the other melting in its river. Cleopatra and Octavia are the pair, Voluptas and Virtus, between whom Hercules must choose; Antony's substance dissolves like a cloud dislimned, like shadow, a sky-show of the dragonish, the bearlike, the lionlike—no longer substance, only a passing show (4.14.1ff).

3. It is hard to believe, but I cannot find that anyone has noticed the use here of the *Life of Caligula.*

It certainly appears that Shakespeare's interest in these twins and divided pairs was exceptional. Spenser uses "shadow," almost always, to mean "shade." It is true that he has his polarity, Una and Duessa, and that one is substance, two or many shadow; he has his twin Florimells, true and false, his double-dealer Archimago. But although his poem is full of feigning and full of shows, Spenser does not make a linguistic issue of them. Donne was more like Shakespeare in this; he loved doubles and splittings, maps arbitrarily divided east and west, coins that not only have twin obverse and reverse but also bear the shadow of the king's face. He likes the baby doubles in lovers' eyes, and those alchemical conjunctions, replications in vitro of a cosmic hermaphroditism. But he chooses his illustrations to feed his transient conceits, he isn't obsessed with them; he hardly exceeds what might be expected of a learned and very witty poet in an age which, perhaps more than most, dwelt on favored sets of opposites: nature and grace, action and contemplation, truth and opinion, the noumenal and the phenomenal. I do not think, however, that one can find anywhere else that passion for what John Carey, discussing Donne,[4] call "joined opposites," which is so evident in Shakespeare, and which reaches a sort of climax in *The Phoenix and Turtle*.

Shakespeare's birds are doubled in their mutual flame; they loved "as love in twain / Had the essence but in one; / Two distincts, division none." They had the quality of transcendent singleness: "Number there in love was slain," for one, the saying went, is no number. Thus, in them alone, the totally single self is mysteriously also another. "Property"—the condition of being single to oneself—is appalled "that the self was not the same." The word *selfsame* is not unusual in Shakespeare, but here it is virtually a *hapax legomenon*, split into *self* and *same*, yet still the selfsame word and still one, containing the notion of selfhood, property, in a novel com-

4. John Donne, *John Donne, His Life and Art* (1981), 264ff.

bination with that of resemblance, which is inconsistent with identity. The scholastic terminology—"property," "distinction" as opposed to "division," "simple" contrasted with "compounded"—is reinforced by ordinary language catachretically twisted into antonymic conjunctions on the model of *selfsame*: "either neither." Alternatives are neutralized without being eliminated in this freakish linguistic optics; they form perspectives, weird shows of almost unimaginable substance.

Plato's hermaphrodite partook of the nature of both sexes but was cut in two, so that the self was not the same; and the divided parts strove to be one in the sense that the broken halves of a coin or of a symbol are one: "two distincts, division none." Within the distincts there is a principle of primal identity, of which we are aware when we look at the halves of an apple, or at twins, or lovers, or the Trinity; or at the phenomena, whether astronomical or rhetorical, that cause us to speak of *concordia discors* or of *discordia concors* in relation to conceits and stars. Neoplatonists and theologians could, by similar means, explain how love unites poverty and plenty, or word and flesh, undivided distincts and neither-eithers.

It is only because language submits to catachresis, or at any rate to metaphorical use and abuse that tend toward that condition, that we can speak at all of these tremendous metaphysical condensations. In *The Phoenix and Turtle* we encounter them in an extraordinarily pure, unqualified form, and we should not expect to find the like in poetry written first for the ear. Yet in the theater there exist all the necessary conditions: it is remote but not asunder, distinct but not divided. The Globe is and is not the globe, it is a shadow of the globe; there is a theatre of the world that does and does not contain the world, "a natural perspective, that is and is not." It's liable always to the irruption of carnival, the opposite of Lenten reality, turning that reality into a play; as Belsey Bob bursts into the Mummers' Play talking like Sir Thopas in *Twelfth Night* but reversing his terms, saying "That that is not."[5] It is in the language of *Hamlet* that we may look for these conjunctures, perspectives, and condensations—for a vast expansion of that serious play given full concentrated expression in *The Phoenix and Turtle,* which was written, as it happens, about the same time as the tragedy.

As we know, attention was for a great while fixed on the character of the hero, at the cost of prolonged inattention to the language of the play as something more than evidence of character, and to those internal relations which are inexplicitly registered in the language. A blend of both sorts of attention may be found in Goethe, but a more decisive change in the conversation (to use Richard Rorty's expression for similar alterations of emphasis in philosophy) cannot be detected until much later, until some half a century ago. We may take "conversation" in the sense—broader than ours but including it—which it still had in Shakespeare's time and beyond— "the action of consorting or having dealings with others; living together, commerce," as the *OED* spells it out. It requires a substantial alteration in the habit of a community for such a change to be licensed, and the change is slowed by conservative persons who sometimes mistake the recent past for the entire tradition. To look closely not at the "psychology" of Lady Macbeth but at the rhetoric of such expressions as "what thou wouldst highly / That wouldst thou holily," and to give the entire text the sort of attention such examples demand, was the aim of L. C. Knights in his *How Many Children Had Lady Macbeth?,* a polemical pamphlet that over fifty years ago announced, though of course it could not of itself consolidate, the change of conversation. And quite independently of Knights, Wilson Knight urged upon us (with the powerful support of T. S. Eliot) an interpretative method that called

5. Sir Thopas's reply to Malvolio's complaint that he is being kept in a dark house, "Why, it hath bay windows transparent as barricadoes, and the clerestories toward the south north are as lustrous as ebony" (4.2.36ff.), is modeled on the carnival-like inversions of Belsey Bob.

for another sort of attention, the kind accorded to canonical books of which it is presupposed that all their parts are occultly interrelated—that they have a "spatial" as well as a temporal mode. Also independently, scholars began to pay more attention to the formal rhetoric of Shakespeare, so that Lady Macbeth's "highly-holily" might be cited as an instance of paronomasia, though of course that is only the first and most obvious thing to say about it in terms of rhetoric. The change in conversation may be expressed thus: the actual language of the play, its very texture, had been treated as a marginal matter, merely as the medium that enabled us to see more important things. Now it could be moved into the center of our interest, and "character" in consequence reduced to relative marginality.

I do not think it would be very useful, though it may well have been done, to list all the rhetorical figures found in *Hamlet:* lots of catachresis, plenty of turpiloquium (when words are "wrung into a filthy sense"),[6] instances of attemperation ("so oft it chanceth in particular men"). This is archaeology. Let us use some of the old terms, but think rather of what it means to give to the holism of Wilson Knight and the poetic attentiveness of L. C. Knights the character of a modern analysis along the lines proposed by Roman Jakobson, who claimed that "poetry sets off the structural elements of all the linguistic levels . . . everything becomes *significant, réciproque, converse, correspondant*";[7] that degree of intensity Jakobson gave to his reading of a sonnet cannot, of course, be matched in a study of *Hamlet,* but we can, as they say, "foreground the utterance," and see what it tells us about the whole.

Broadly speaking, the central rhetorical device of *Hamlet* is doubling. This is partly an echo of the period rhetoric; we are

6. L. Sonnino, *A Handbook to Sixteenth-Century Rhetoric* (1968), 188 (quoting Richard Sherry).

7. Roman Jakobson, *Selected Writings, III: Poetry of Grammar and Grammar of Poetry* (1981), 767.

familiar with it from the *Book of Common Prayer,* in which sixteenth-century English finds its own vernacular equivalent for a liturgy long entrusted to Latin, and needing some differentiation from ordinary language. "We acknowledge and confess our manifold sins and wickednesses," runs the General Confession; it gets some of its effect from reduplication that mimes the multiple guilt of many sinners speaking together, and more, possibly, from the sense that to *acknowledge* is not quite the same as to *confess,* and that *sins* are theologically a bit more specific than *wickednesses.* In much the same way "spare thou them, O God, which confess their faults, restore thou them that are penitent" reminds us of the Psalmist's *parallelismus membrorum,* yet within its doubling there is a slight discrepancy of sense, for to be spared and to be restored are not exactly the same thing, and even though it is harder to distinguish between being penitent and confessing, the second cannot occur without the first nor the first, properly, without the second, so that they are distincts without division; and even if they were not, even if they were identical in sense, their identity would be a contribution to the meaning of the whole, for as Hoskins remarks in his *Directions for Speech and Style* (a work exactly contemporary with *Hamlet*), "in speech there is no repetition without importance."[8]

Although *Hamlet* contains a good deal of rather expansive doubling along these lines, the most pregnant and interesting of its linguistic doublings is undoubtedly hendiadys. This is the figure which, as its name implies, expresses "one through two," as when Virgil says *pateris libamus et auro,* "we drink from cups and gold" instead of "we drink from golden cups." This figure occurs with remarkable frequency in *Hamlet,* and had not altogether escaped attention, but it seems significant of the changing nature of our conversation that the first systematic study of it did not appear until 1981. This was George T. Wright's "Hendiadys and *Hamlet*" (*PMLA* 96,

8. Sonnino, 157, quoting J. Hoskins, *Direction for Speech and Style* (c. 1600).

168ff.), an article that not only repairs the neglect of former commentary but is in its own right a brilliant piece of literary criticism. The trick at its simplest is to conjoin two distinct words in the expression of a single idea, as in "ponderous and marble jaws"; but as the Virgilian example suggests, the combination may be much more forced than that, and the separateness of the conjoined ideas as important as their capacity for conjunction. "Ponderous" and "marble" could easily be distinct epithets alike appropriate to the "jaws" of a sepulchre (in fact they emphasise that "jaws" is also a figure: graves "swallow" people and so have jaws, but really the jaws are heavy pieces of marble, etc.). But "the perfume and suppliance of a minute" (Laertes describing Hamlet's courtship of Ophelia, 1.3.9) is more complicated, because the suppliance— "entertainment," "passing the time" or such—has got itself scented by the perfume, and the perfume cannot work at all without the suppliance; "the perfume of a minute" doesn't sound right, as "ponderous jaws" or "marble jaws" sound right. As Wright remarks, hendiadys can introduce unease and mystery by means of what Eliot called, in another connection, "a perpetual slight alteration of language"—by deviations, by doing something other than we expect from words joined by "and," by a sort of violation of the promise of simple parataxis. The effect is comparable to that of zeugma (an unexpected yoking: "she left in a flood of tears and a sedan chair") where one verb syntactically serves two sentence ideas, so that the logical structure, like that of the metaphysical conceit, is close to that of a joke.

However, as Wright further remarks, hendiadys isn't funny; its conjunctions of distincts are apt to produce unease. And it had, as Wright definitively demonstrates, a peculiar fascination for Shakespeare in a period lasting for a few years after 1599. That is to say, it coincides, accidentally or not, with the company's move to the Globe, which tempts me to guess that the flag or emblem of the theatre, "Hercules and his load," meaning the world, the theater as the world, may itself be read as a hendiadys ("Hercules' load"). *Hamlet,* the most self-proclaiming theatrical of all the plays, also has far more instances of this trope than any other play—sixty-six by Wright's careful and conservative count, more than twice as many as *Othello*, the next tragedy and easily second to *Hamlet* in this respect.

Wright's criterion for hendiadys is a certain interplay between the parts, so that the figure takes far more explication than you might expect to have to provide. "The sensible and true avouch / Of mine own eyes" (1.1.57) means something like "the sensorily accurate testimony of my eyes to what I could not have believed on mere report," the first adjective modifying the second rather than modifying "avouch." Wright finds such instances of hendiadys exactly expressive of the "deceptive linkings" characteristic of the play as a whole, and he makes a very good case for this view.

My only reservation is that in his scrupulous attempt to distinguish between hendiadys and other forms of doubling Wright tends to exclude the remainder from consideration, though they obviously have a lot to do with the tone and working of the play; it is possible even that there is a sort of hierarchy of doublets, with hendiadys as the most complex and the most central. At any rate, what is reflected at all levels is not just hendiadys but doubling. Cornelius and Voltemand are indistinguishable, distincts without division; one of them would have served very well. Rosencrantz and Guildenstern are a double cherry, a union in partition. The play-within-the-play is an uneasy double of *Hamlet,* and the dumbshow an imperfect shadow or show of the play-within-the-play. Whenever something can be doubled, it is: revenges and revengers, lawful espials, ghostly visitations. The chronography of Barnardo:

> Last night of all
> When yon same star that's westward from the pole,
> Had made his course t'illume that part of heaven
> Where now it burns. . . . (1.1.38–41)

is doubled by Horatio's chronography at the end of the scene:

> But look, the morn in russet mantle clad
> Walks o'er the dew of yon high eastward hill (1.1.171–72)

and these two flourishes enclose like parentheses the excursus of Marcellus on Christmas ("so hallow'd and so gracious is that time" [1.1.169]). Laertes, himself a shadow or show of Hamlet, has a double departure and is twice blessed by his father ("A double blessing is a double grace" [1.3.53]); and so forth. These compulsive duplications occur everywhere, and with varying effect. Sometimes they are simple, as when they underline the orotund vacuity of Polonius:

> And thus do we of wisdom and of reach,
> With windlasses and with assays of bias
> By indirection find directions out.
> So by my former lecture and advice
> Shall you my son. You have me, have you not? (2.1.64–68)

(The effect is not unlike that of Othello's talk at the beginning of that play.) Or Ophelia's inadequacy:

> . . . Th'expectancy and rose of the fair state,
> The glass of fashion and the mould of form,
> Th'observ'd of all observers, quite, quite down!
> And I of ladies most deject and wretched,
> That suck'd the music of his honey'd vows,
> Now see that noble and most sovereign reason
> Like sweet bells jangled out of tune and harsh,
> That unmatch'd form and feature of blown youth
> Blasted with ecstasy. (3.1.154–62)

Every line here save one contains doublets. Rosencrantz and Guildenstern dispose them in their courtier-like moments ("The single and peculiar life is bound / With all the strength and armour of the mind," etc. [3.3.11ff.]); but so does Hamlet in his soliloquies. These doublings, which of course include the strangest and most figurative of doublings, hendiadys, are simply the habit of the play.

Before we consider more of them in detail, it will be con-
venient to have some central principle of doubling in mind. It
may be said that the play is deeply concerned with two main
sorts of doubling. One is the doubling of theater and world,
the theater as mirror in which actors are shadows or reflections and, when they play the parts of actors, shadows of
shadows. The other great doubling is marriage, and marriage
in the peculiarly intense and maximally intimate form of
incest.

The funeral of a king, and the marriage of his widow to
another king, his brother, is a doubling that prompts Hamlet's
sour joke about doubling the wedding breakfast with the funeral feast; the unnatural temporal proximity of these functions
reflects the physical proximity of incestuous marriage. Two
persons becoming one is a form of thrift in which the self ceases
to be the same, and what ought to be distinct is not divided.
When Hamlet says, in bidding the King goodbye, "Farewell,
dear mother," the King corrects him: "Thy loving father,
Hamlet." But Hamlet knows what he is saying, his logic is the
logic of two-as-one: "My mother. Father and mother is man
and wife, man and wife is one flesh; so my mother" (4.3.52–
54). He disallows distinction where there is no division: marriage, and especially incestuous marriage, this particular beast
with two backs, is a kind of hermaphroditism, or, if the catachresis is permitted, a social hendiadys containing mystery and
unease, displaying a one that seems concordant but is not so, or
is too much so, the kinship of aunt-mother and uncle-father
being excessive; one might speak, even more disgustingly, of
aunt-father and uncle-mother. Pondering this kinship relation,
Hamlet also calls his mother her "husband's brother's wife"
(3.4.14), which, accurate as it is, stresses the position of the
marriage outside the permitted degrees of consanguinity,
though at the same time it represents the compound relation as
a horribly single one. Hamlet's first line, "A little more than
kin and less than kind" (1.2.65) is almost a textbook paronomasia; it depends upon the resemblance of one word to

another. "Kin" and "kind" are an imperfect doublet, related phonetically, orthographically, and semantically, yet also distinct in all these ways, and represented as antithetical, thus stressing the horrible disparities implied by so close and profane a union.

Incest is equivocal (husband-wife, brother-sister) and breeds equivocation ("my cousin Hamlet and my son . . . Our chiefest courtier, cousin and our son" [1.2.64, 117]); the repetition is not merely redundant, for it makes the usurpation of Claudius a multiple one ("think of us / As of a father")—the "us" and "our" are royal plurals. All these piled up doubles, whether hendiadys or not, must create a sense of oddness and uneasiness when seen in their context, the huge equivoques of the whole scheme. They can be ignored or treated as occult, as having to do with secrecy rather than sense (see 3.4.194), but it is proper enough, on occasion, to defy the defense mechanism by which we ordinarily suppress knowledge of them.

It would be impossible to list, let alone discuss, all the doublings of this text, so here is a list drawn from the first 180 lines of the play, with some comment.

a) *You tremble and look pale.* (ordinary language)
b) I might not this believe
   Without *the sensible and true avouch*
   Of mine own eyes. (hendiadys: see above) (approved by Wright)
c) . . . in *the gross and scope of my opinion* (hendiadys: "full extent") (Wright)
d) *Strict and most observant watch* (close and observant; but close to "strictly observant," "strictly kept," and so a near-hendiadys)
e) . . . *ratified by law and heraldry* (hendiadys, according to Wright—"heraldic law"; but not much more so than "Strict and most observant")
f) by the same *cov'nant / And carriage* of the article (hen-

diadys; glossed by Arden editor as "purport of the article"; the agreement as carried out [?])

g) unimproved mettle, *hot and full* (hendiadys: "full of heat")

h) *food and diet* (simple duplication)

i) *post-haste and rummage* ("hurry and turmoil"; but a pair, surely, a nonce-formation on the model of helter-skelter, hugger-mugger, handy-dandy, hurly-burly; and a sort of hendiadys)

j) *high and palmy* (palmily high? highly palmy?)

k) *squeak and gibber* (a composite representation of the sound ghosts make? a pair, not two distincts?)

l) *trains of fire and dews of blood* (parallelism of members)

m) And even the like *precurse* of fear'd events
   As *harbingers* preceding still the fates
   And *prologue* to the *omen* coming on
   Have *heaven and earth* together demonstrated
   Unto our *climatures and countrymen*. (highly repetitive: "precurse," "harbingers," "prologue," "omen"—and possibly also "preceding"—form a very redundant series, each doubling the others, and the simple pair "heaven and earth," partnered by the stranger conjunction "climatures and countrymen," meaning something like "the inhabitants of our region," brings the sequence to a close)

n) *If thou hast any sound or use of voice* (uncertain as to the kind of response that might be expected, neither "sound" nor "use of voice" commits him to an expectation of human speech; the Ghost might squeak and gibber; here again is a pair in the general ambience of hendiadys, without quite fitting acceptable definitions)

o) That may do *ease* to *you* and *grace* to *me* (here "ease" and "grace" is a double divided, shared out one each)

p) *Lofty and shrill sounding* throat ("lofty throat" would be a little forced; the second epithet glosses the first)

q) Th'*extravagant and erring* spirit ("extravagant" and "erring" are an apparently exact double, but there are semantic undercurrents that hold them apart; cf. *Othello*, "extravagant and wheeling stranger" [1.1.136] and "For nature so preposterously to err" [1.3.62])

r) *So hallow'd and so gracious* is that time (holy because the means of grace)

Of the eighteen passages here listed, Wright allows as true instances of hendiadys only the three I have indicated. In a supplementary list of "phrases that, if not hendiadys, are close, or odd" but which he felt he must, "in the last analysis, reject," he includes four more: *strict and most observant, hot and full, food and diet,* and *post-haste and rummage.* It would be a task of some delicacy to grade the hundreds of doubles in the language of *Hamlet,* to measure their oddity and their closeness to the oddest and sovereign figure of hendiadys. What is certain is that the cumulative effect is very intense and also very various. If the garrulous doublings of Polonius are on the whole comic, the same cannot be said of the doubled language of 1.5. There, the Ghost says he must render himself up to "sulph'rous and tormenting flames"; he must have his foul crimes "burnt and purg'd away." His full story, if he told it, would not only harrow Hamlet's soul but also freeze his blood; it would make his hair, which is at once knotted and combined (like the words used to describe it) both part and stand on end. However, he cannot unfold his tale to ears of flesh and blood. His murder was both foul and most unnatural, and his murderer a man both incestuous and adulterate. The poison employed courses through the gates (or wider streets) of his body, but also through its alleys, curdling the thin, therefore wholesome, blood, and covering him with a vile, that was also a loathsome, crust. His bed became a couch for luxury *and* damned incest—a hendiadys of sorts, the incest being luxurious makes it doubly damnable, the luxury being incestuous makes it more luxurious. Hamlet replies with a flurry of doublets: "trivial fond records," "youth and observation" (a classic hendiadys), "the book and volume" of his brain. Meeting his friends again, he urges them twice to pursue their business and desires; Horatio joins in, remarking on Hamlet's "wild and whirling words," which is paronomasia as well as doubling; and then, after all the excitement, the doublets dwindle to the commonplace but basic "heaven and earth," "grace and mercy," "love and friending."

Before those words are spoken, we have had one of those passages of rapid dialogue—no time for doubling—which sometimes vary the rhythms of this incomparable poem; and there are other long moments during which doubling, by its mere absence, helps in the establishment of a different tone. One such passage is the prose conversation between Hamlet and the newly arrived Rosencrantz and Guildenstern in 2.2; as we have seen, the spy-sycophants are perfectly capable of courtly duplication and duplicity ("Heaven makes our presence and our practices / Pleasant and helpful to him" [2.2.38–39]); but in response to Hamlet's unaffected greeting they drop what in them is a courtly device, and the candor of the conversation in which Hamlet discovers their mission is reinforced. The more effective, then, is the doubling in the famous speech "I have of late . . . lost all my mirth, forgone all custom of exercise" (2.2.295ff.), and Hamlet's allusion, as the conversation ends, to "fashion and ceremony," and to his "uncle-father and aunt-mother" (2.2.368ff.).

Such instances, and the doublings of Polonius, more art than matter, make it impossible to speak of the device as if it had a single purpose. It isn't, for example, the case that it is always excluded from prose scenes. Hamlet's prose when he speaks of the players is very receptive of doubles: he calls the actors "the abstract and brief chronicles of the time" ([2.2.520]: Wright, preferring to read "abstracts" with F1 and Q1, classifies this as hendiadys). He later says they will show "the very age and body of the time his form and pressure" ([3.2.23–24]: "age . . . time" is hendiadys for Wright); they should not strut and bellow, but they should "suit the action to the word" (3.2.17)—a pairing too often, in his view, parted. Not surprisingly, then, the Player's account of Priam has him falling at the "whiff and wind" of Pyrrhus's sword (2.2.469); and, not surprisingly, the soliloquy that concludes this remarkable scene begins as it means to continue: "O what a rogue and peasant slave am I" (2.2.544). We shall hear of fiction and dream, motive and cue, of a speaker dull and muddy-mettled. He had a father "Upon whose property and most dear life / A damn'd defeat was made" (the appalling of property). He is "pigeon-liver'd" and "lacks gall" (the second expression explaining the first, since pigeons were thought to have livers without gall). He unpacks his heart with words like a whore, and curses like a drab. However, he has a plot which will serve the single yet double purpose of testing king and Ghost—each of whom is a king, and each of whom is his father.

Here as elsewhere it is the variety of effect that gives the poetry its character. The mechanical doublets of Ophelia (expectancy and rose, glass of fashion, mold of form, observed and observer, deject and wretched, jangled, out of tune, etc.) contrast vividly with the powerful, anxious hendiadys in the King's speech immediately following:

> There's something in his soul
> O'er which his melancholy sits on brood,
> And I do doubt the hatch and the disclose
> Will be some danger . . . (3.1.166ff.)

This has to be glossed as "that which will be disclosed when it hatches" or in some equally unsatisfactory way; it is a very good example of the linguistic disturbance this form of doubling entails, an image of the anxieties that the play broods over. A simple double like the Queen's exclamation at the death of Polonius, "O what a rash and bloody deed is this!" (3.4.27) may begin a train of very complex ones: "A bloody deed, / Almost as bad, good mother, / As kill a king and marry with his brother" (28–29), where "good" seems to stand antithetically to "bad" but is yoked, with ironic conventionality, and in Hamlet's view inappropriately, with "mother"; where "kill" and "marry" form a wicked pair, and where the rhyme of "mother" and "brother" mimes the too rich rhyme of incest. The Closet scene, indeed, is full of such conundrums, far too many to mention: form and cause, scourge and minister, sense and secrecy. Hamlet's final soliloquy, "How all occasions . . ." (4.4.32ff.), anomalous as its position certainly is, nevertheless forms a kind of coda, recapitulating the theme thus: good and market, sleep and feed, before and after, capability and godlike reason, bestial oblivion and craven scruple, mass and charge, fantasy and trick, tomb and continent, delicate and tender, mortal and unsure. The crux at 1.54 ("Rightly to be great / Is not to stir without great argument, / But greatly to find quarrel in a straw / When honour's at the stake") turns on the question of whether "not" should properly be "not not," one not doing the work of two, two negatives in a single mutual flame.

This, then, is a play in which self is sometimes joined with, sometimes divided from, same; opposites are conjoined and similars separated. Why is Horatio both familiar and a stranger? Why are we to be troubled with the question whether the Ghost is honest or not? Why should Hamlet double his abuse of woman, and berate Ophelia as he does his mother? Why, having persuaded her of her guilt, turned her eyes into her very soul, does he double his condemnations? Having cleft her heart in twain, why does he repeat his lecture on abstinence? Why is he doubly mad or not mad at all? A shadow of the actor who is himself but a shadow? Why, in short, is the play so often like a pair of twins, a divided hermaphrodite? The restoration of the primal hermaphrodite, according to Aristophanes in the *Symposium,* is attempted by the divided halves when, their private parts moved around to the front, they make the beast with two backs, when, in the rank sweat of an enseamed bed they reunite, touch, as *The Winter's Tale* expresses it, forbiddenly.

We can say, at any rate, that in the year or so that was occupied by the writing of *Hamlet, The Phoenix and Turtle,* and *Twelfth Night,* Shakespeare not only developed his taste for doublets, including the incestuous doublet of hendiadys—a

development for which much in his earlier practice has pre-
pared us—but took to extraordinary lengths his interest in
twinning, male and female, in the self and the same, the self
that is not the same. There are the great antithetical doublings of the social life, Carnival and Lent, and all the other
traditional opposites that make unions—one and number,
knowledge and opinion, noumena and phenomena, substance
and shadow; and they are reflected in the language of poetry
as rhyme (either-neither, mother-brother) or assonance, or
pun or hendiadys. Thematically they may emerge as the perspective of twins, or the one flesh of marriage and incest.
Together, these things make a mirror of a world that is one,
but built on a principle of opposition in all its structures.

Of that opposition, substance-and-shadow is a primeval
figure. In folklore, to lose one's shadow is to be castrated or
made infertile. In some languages, the same word does duty
for "soul" and "shadow,"[9] so that images and reflections are
also projections of the soul. Mirrors are not to be broken; in
times of mourning they are covered. In Lacan's *stade du miroir*
we have our modern version of such spiritual disasters.

One's image or double may also be a rival, as son of father;
the act of doubling is itself a reflex of the oedipal theme.
Sisters may be the doubles of brothers; Narcissus mistook his
reflection for his sister. The Duke in *Twelfth Night* thinks of
Sebastian and Viola as a perspective, two in one, and Antonio
says that a cleft apple is not more twin than they, but they are
distinct also, and opposed; Viola thinks her brother a spirit
"come to fright us" (5.1.236). Shakespeare's twins Hamnet
and Judith were born in 1585; Hamnet died in 1596, the year
of the twin plays *Romeo and Juliet* and *A Midsummer Night's
Dream*.

It has been argued by a follower of D. W. Winnicott that a
twin may take the place of more usual transitional objects but
may be a poor substitute, being too like the mother, animate;

9. Otto Rank, *The Double,* trans. Harry Tucker, Jr. (1971; 1979 ed.), 58.

so that the move from inner to outer reality is impeded—there may be difficulty in achieving the required decathexis.[10] However that may be, there are fantasy twins as well as real ones. Hamlet's hypercathexis on his father has often been noticed; the true father was the substance of his shadow, and the defeat of his "property" left Hamlet not with that substance but with its evil replacement, the shadow-king, shadow-husband, and shadow-father, Claudius. His mother splits in two; wife to both "this" and "this," her self is no longer the same, and Hamlet is appalled in the name of Property. In the catachresis of *The Phoenix and Turtle* and the perspective of *Twelfth Night*, we may see a concentrated version of that multilevel doubling and twinning that *Hamlet* expands to its full theatrical dimensions in the Globe, which is itself the shadow of the world's substance.

These remarks about *Hamlet* imply certain assumptions. Different as they are from the great bulk of past commentary, they have something in common with the way critics nowadays often talk. The main line of approach is rhetorical; not that I have sought to specify all the varieties of trope, merely using instances here and there, and not seeking, as Wright's admirable study sought, to distinguish sharply between hendiadys and other forms of doubling, or to study the many types of paronomasia to be found in the text. The assumption is, of course, that I might look anywhere in the play (in the "world of the play," as we not inaccurately say) for resemblances suggested by my guiding idea, and that here, as Henry James remarked in another connection, "relations stop nowhere."

---

10. D. Parish, "Transitional Objects and Phenomena in a Case of Twinship," *Between Fantasy and Reality*, ed. S. A. Goalnick and L. Barkin (1978), 273–87. The case described is of a neurotic younger dizygotic twin who had a tendency "to view separate people as halves of dyads," especially when he wanted to reject them; however, he mistrusted this feeling. Hamlet certainly tends to think of the dead and living kings as a dyad, and wishes to reject the latter.

Here they will sometimes appear to subsist between the obvious and the farfetched, or, to be more generous to myself, between the manifest and the latent.

Assumptions of that sort are characteristically made about canonical texts, texts that share with the sacred at least this quality: that however a particular epoch or a particular community may define a proper mode of attention or a licit area of interest, there will always be something else and something different to say. There is, of course, room for dissent within the agreement that the last word cannot be said, but it is hard to suppose that there can be progress ensured by the testing of hypotheses; all we are sure about is that the inadequacies of earlier exposition become astonishingly obvious to later expositors, that there can be no simple and perpetual consensus as to the proper way to join the shadow of comment to the substance of the play. And this is what it means to call a book canonical. The game is in a sense the same one that Goethe and Coleridge played, but the rules change, and we know it is the same game only by reason of family resemblance: all grant to the text something like omnisignificance, all have canons of interpretation that are permissive rather than restrictive. Relations must appear to stop somewhere, and some views as to where they ought to stop are stricter than others, though they are views that are themselves mere opinions and not the certainties that they are sometimes taken for. Above all, the reason why friend and foe are both able to do as they wish, and to recognize that in the end their discourses are of the same sort, is that *Hamlet* is unshakably canonical—the dislodgment of such a work from canonical status would certainly involve the dislodgment of those discourses, of whatever party. In short, the only rule common to all interpretation games, the sole family resemblance between them, is that the canonical work, so endlessly discussed, must be assumed to have permanent value and, which is really the same thing, perpetual modernity.

As I was writing this, a man told me his dream. He dreamed that, being overweight, he dieted and became slender, feeling that in doing so he had acquired an entirely new personality.

Then, in his new body, he had a dream within the dream, and in this inner dream he saw himself as he had been originally— much fatter, but somehow more at home in his ampler shape. Still dreaming, the sleeper decided to act on this hint, and resume his former, bulkier shape. On waking he found he had done so; he awoke and found it truth. He had, in the outer dream, reduced himself to a shadow of his former self, and in the inner regained his substance.

This reminded me not only that Hamlet, young and fit at the beginning of the play is, at the end of it, after his lapse in time and passion, fat and thirty, but also that his play is a fiction, a dream of passion, in which there are dreams within dreams, and mirror on mirror mirrored is all the show. Moreover, the conversations of interpreters are shadows or images, fat or thin, and not matters of substance, except that where there is shadow there must be substance, and a light on it; so the end of all this shadowy talk is after all to keep a real and valued object in being. That, to offer one more hendiadys, is my sense of the play and duty of interpretation; but there is more to be said of it, and that will be the substance of what, follows.

3

3

*Disentangling
Knowledge
from Opinion*

It is now time to consider some of the implications of my remarks on Botticelli and *Hamlet*. The most obvious is this: that the preservation of canonical works is achieved by means of argument that may not be truly worthy of that name, and which is, at best, incapable of resisting later criticism. Mostly, indeed, it disappears spontaneously, denied even the honor of judicial execution. It becomes part of that which it is normal to reject, a necessary condition of modernity itself, considered as "the ever renewed attempt at self-definition by rejection of a past."[1]

The success of interpretative argument as a means of conferring or endorsing value is, accordingly, not to be measured by the survival of the comment but by the survival of its object. Of course, an interpretation or evaluation may live on in the tradition on which later comment is formed, either by acceptance or reaction; but its primary purpose is to provide the medium in which its object survives.

The relative ignorance of his proponents proved no obstacle to the canonization of Botticelli. The work of Warburg and Horne, which was done when the position had already been established, may be thought of as belonging to a period of consolidation; and it was by contrast very learned work. Here relatively speaking was knowledge, where formerly, in the commentary of the first wave of Botticellians, there was mere opinion.

The distinction between knowledge and opinion is ancient and variously stated, so I should try to say how far I have found it serviceable in the present discussion. Then I will ask whether there are important differences between the sort of knowledge Horne used and the more systematic and speculative knowledge of Warburg. What, in this context, are the uses of system? What are the justifications of the direct Horneian approach, which, roughly speaking, assumes that nothing stands between the researcher and his documents, and

1. H. R. Jauss, *Aesthetic Experience and Literary Hermeneutics*, trans. Michael Shaw (1982), 260.

Chapter Three

that true valuations depend upon the full understanding thus achieved? And, finally, I should ask not only how the canon is preserved by the multiple action of various sorts of opinion, knowledge, and mixtures of the two, but why it is and whether it ought to be.

> The systems of learning . . . must be sometimes reviewed, complications analysed into principles, and knowledge disentangled from opinion. It is not always possible, without close inspection, to separate the genuine shoots of consequential learning, which grow out of some radical postulate, from the branches which have been engrafted upon it. The accidental prescriptions of authority, when time has procured them veneration, are often confounded with the laws of nature, and those rules supposed coeval with reason, of which the first rise cannot be discovered . . . It ought to be the first endeavour of a writer to distinguish between nature and custom, and that which is established because it is right from that which is right only because it is established.[2]

As usual, Dr. Johnson sounds authoritative. Though he affirms so strongly the requirement that nature be distinguished from custom and knowledge from opinion, his conceptual apparatus is customary enough, and the hierarchical distinctions—nature preferred to custom and knowledge to opinion—are themselves rooted in custom and opinion. Johnson moreover assumes that systems of learning need revision, rather than replacement by some new "radical postulate." That some of the prescriptions of authority may have an imperfect claim upon us in no way entails the consequence that all of them are faulty; some are established because they are right, and it is our business not to reject them all but to decide which are right and which are not.

As a program, this is undeniably attractive. Who would not wish to expose that which merely preserves an appearance of being reasonable, and can do so only because of the inherited

2. Samuel Johnson, *Rambler*, no. 156 (September 14, 1751).

difficulty of putting it to the question? What scholar of spirit
would refuse the challenge, the demand that he or she lift the
load of custom? Disentangle knowledge from opinion? Yet
the prudent may well want first to consider some of the conse-
quences of doing so. For example, what would have happened
if, much earlier than Horne, somebody had disentangled
knowledge from opinion in the new celebration of Botticelli?
Perhaps the revival, fueled as it was by ignorant enthusiasm,
would never have happened. And it will probably seem to us
far more difficult than Johnson thought to distinguish what is
established because it is right from what is right because it is
established. In the matter of canonicity the antithesis col-
lapses; its two halves are merely two ways of saying the same
thing. And yet there perhaps remains *some* difference between
knowledge and opinion.

There are various estimates of the value of opinion, even
within the works of Plato, who frequently, though not always
in precisely the same way, distinguished it from knowledge.
He says it is not the same as ignorance, but always maintains
its inferiority to knowledge. Socrates, indeed, maintains (*Re-
public* VI.506e) that opinions divorced from knowledge are
ugly things, and that even to hold a true opinion unin-
telligently is to be like the blind man going the right way. The
Stoics held the opinion that opinion is always and entirely bad,
a view vigorously endorsed by those who revived their philosophy in the Renaissance. Pascal, in the *Pensées*,[3] sketches an
extraordinarily tortuous argument which suggests, among
other things, that sound opinion held in ignorance of the truth
is in fact unsound opinion, which is really the same point as
that of Socrates; but he adds that a great man who has ac-
quainted himself with all knowledge, and is thus able to distinguish it from opinion, is for all that aware that he knows
nothing except this one thing, which alone distinguishes him
from the ignorant or opinionated. Pascal shows as well as
anyone could how hard it is, even on "close inspection," to

3. Pascal, *Pensées*, ed. and trans. A. J. Krailsheimer (1966), 89–93.

disentangle knowledge from opinion, and how little there is left of the "systems of learning" when one has done so.

Of the operation of opinion in the fortunes of artists and works of art, it can be said that it may be preservative and it may be destructive. So far, we have been looking at the preservative aspect. Speaking of Botticelli and the extraordinary revival of his fortunes in the nineteenth century, I expressed the opinion that it was largely the work of opinion. "What is aught but as 'tis valued?" Herbert Horne more than once suggested, as we saw, that the revaluation was to a considerable extent based on work that was not by Botticelli at all but by imitators whose style had a greater appeal than the master's to tastes Horne thought corrupt. And so you might say that Horne's great knowledge came into play when he formed certain opinions that made it possible to put into the space reserved for the veneration of Botticelli works of which he could demonstrate the authenticity, and which might thenceforth benefit from the adulation formerly excited by the spurious. So in any case, recognition of the greatness of Botticelli depended in the first place on erroneous opinion; error is the inescapable shadow of opinion. Yet we saw that shadow lying however faintly across Horne's own work, and across Warburg's also.

Historians of art could cite other instances of the same process, Caravaggio perhaps, and in music there is the notable case of Monteverdi; literary history is not without examples equally remarkable. One such is the reputation of John Donne, whose peculiar fortunes have been excellently recounted by Joseph E. Duncan.[4] Donne's fame, like Botticelli's, began to wane very early. Attempts were made to preserve it in an epoch professing different standards, and having different notions about excellence, but even in the early seventeenth century they have a somewhat desperate air, as when a commentator argues that "The Good Morrow" is not a wickedly erotic poem but an address to God; and that the

4. Joseph E. Duncan, *The Revival of Metaphysical Poetry* (1959).

lesbian epistle "Sappho to Philaenis" is an allegory of the relationship between Christ and his church. This is a highly traditional method of saving erotic poetry for the canon; it was used by Aqiba to save the Song of Songs in the first century A.D., when its constituent lyrics were still, it seems, sung in the most secular manner in wine shops. But this time it did not work, and quite soon a more down-to-earth form of criticism, as applied by Hobbes and Dryden, for instance, made Donne's case desperate. Dr. Johnson looked at him in his *Life of Cowley*, but his interest was in large part antiquarian and, for the rest, a desire to replace an old concept of wit with a more modern one. Far from enjoying the perpetual modernity accorded to canonical works, the poetry of Donne had come to seem merely quaint and out of touch with the tradition, as that tradition was formed by a later system of learning.

Donne's revival occurred at the same time as Botticelli's, though more slowly and with less impact on the public at large. It depended upon a similar reappraisal of a past now thought to have been undervalued by intervening generations, each partially blinded by its own prejudices—each, that is, mistaking its custom for nature and its opinion for knowledge. A new view of the creative faculty, a new understanding that ratiocination might be the ally rather than the enemy of passion, a new understanding of history, transforming the old opinion about the late Middle Ages and the Renaissance—all these were necessary preliminaries to the restoration of Donne. It was also necessary that these transformations become mere matters of opinion; familiar ground to a reading public, not just a learned coterie.

It was not that Donne was properly understood, even at the level of the "plain" or "grammatical" sense. Indeed, it was virtually impossible to achieve even that measure of understanding before Grierson published his edition in 1912. This was a work in some ways equivalent to Horne's *Botticelli*, published four years earlier. After Grierson's edition, what Donne wrote was for the most part accessible and open to

71

interpretation. But the great work might never have been projected had there not developed so strong an opinion of the merit of these poems, an opinion partly founded in their seemingly impenetrable mysteriousness. Removing the corruptions, Grierson removed some of the excitement; but the notion that the poems demonstrated the possibility of a union of thinking and feeling, and of an end to the modern divorce between these, survived their demystification. It was to this idea that T. S. Eliot lent his authority in 1921, sketching a theory of poetry, and of the canon of poetry, to support it.

So, for a time, Donne became a model of modern "sensibility." When Eliot, changing his position somewhat, described the Donne vogue as "an affair of the present and the recent past rather than of the future," he was inexplicitly but correctly assigning that vogue to the province of opinion. The systematization of the "dissociation of sensibility" was left to the academics; it got under way just when Eliot himself was losing interest. Donne, like Botticelli, has settled into a place in our canon; but we can now see that his admission was peculiarly the work of a past epoch, an effort controlled by historical conditions we identify as quite other than our own. Permanent modernity is conferred on chosen works by arguments and persuasions that cannot, themselves, remain modern. Botticelli and Donne are still highly esteemed, though the original tone of ecstasy has been somewhat muted, and the errors and misunderstandings of their first proponents are part of the record. That the preservation and renewal of these masters has become the duty not of artists and enthusiasts, carefree adherents of opinion, but of canon-defending, theory-laden professors, is a fact of some importance.

Opinion, then, may act as a preservative. That it also has a destructive force is a fact both obvious, and, in discussions of value in the arts, neglected—perhaps understandably, for it is hard to talk about what does not exist, and titles like C. J. Sisson's *Lost Plays of Shakespeare's Age* have a rather recherché ring. But it remains true that opinion can be the ally of chance. Chance may act before opinion can, taking a hand in determining the survival of whatever it is that we may hold opinions about.

For some reason, it is easier to say that an artist has a *fortuna* in other languages than in English; we may speak of his or her "fortunes," but the word sounds awkward, and we tend to avoid it even when using the concept. But of books one can say what Machiavelli said of men, that they are confronted by Fortune with an irreducible element of opposition, described by him as chaos, fatality, necessity, and ignorance. And while men can resist Fortune with some hope of success by the exercise of Virtue, books and mere *objets de vertu*, lacking the *virtù* of men, are in themselves wholly vulnerable to loss and decay, neglect, and iconoclasm. We know of many books which no effort of virtue or opinion can ever restore to our attention—a hundred and sixteen plays of Sophocles, for instance, rejected by second-century pedagogues for perhaps no better reason than that the remaining seven fit into a single codex, designed for use in schools. These survivors were again threatened with extinction during the big switch from uncial to minuscule script in the ninth century; anything not selected for transcription was likely to be lost. And, once again, five hundred years later they needed another bit of luck, and got it when somebody shipped a single copy to Italy only a few years before the catastrophic sack of Constantinople in 1453. Aeschylus was also whittled down from over seventy plays to seven; an attempt was made to reduce his canon even further, to three. Two, the *Eumenides* and the *Agamemnon*, were retrieved in Byzantium, but the remaining two, the *Supplices* and the *Choephoroi*, survived in a single manuscript that also, fortunately, reached Italy in the fifteenth century. Euripides did a bit better, but apparently only by chance.[5]

5. For succinct accounts of the transmission of the texts of Sophocles, Aeschylus, and Euripides, see Sophocles, *Philoctetes,* ed. Webster (1970), Appendix 2 (P. E. Easterling), 164–73; Aeschylus, *Agamemnon,* ed. Denniston and Page (1957), xxxvi–xxxix; Euripides, *Bacchae,* ed. E. R. Dodds (1960), li–lix.

That a book may be a monument *aere perennius* is a conceit, though it happens to be true in a few fortunate cases. Sacred writings inscribed on exceptionally durable materials and too holy to be trashed may, given an exceptional climate, survive, like the Qumran scrolls or the Gnostic writings of Nag Hammadi, though when people stopped talking about them they were as good as dead for the better part of two thousand years. Some books live on only as fossils in the polemic of their opponents, as the Gnostics did in the writings of the victorious Catholic fathers.

Statues may be recovered by excavation or dragged from the sea, jewelry found in tombs, paintings in attics; but virtue comes into play (in the guise of opinion or knowledge) only after that, when the objects need to be recognized, conserved, and talked about. Opinion probably condemned them in the first place. Prejudiced preferences form a large part of the history of art and of documents. The schoolmasters and professors who abolished most of Greek tragedy were, as the saying goes, only doing their job. It is well, then, to remember that opinion is not always on the side of virtue, that it can be a means to oblivion as well as the main defense against it.

Perhaps, indeed, one ought not so sharply to distinguish its two functions; for the perpetuity of one object often entails the oblivion of another. Opinion is the great canon-maker, and you can't have privileged insiders without creating outsiders, apocrypha. The attention of those learned (but still opinionated) communities who assume responsibility for the continuance and modernity of the canon is naturally fixed on the insiders, and the others are allowed to fall under the rule of time, to become merely historical. For one reason or another they may continue to exist, but because the attention they attract is sporadic and relatively unengaged, their state is at best that of half-life; they too are the victims of chance and opinion. Continuity of attention and interpretation, denied to them, is reserved for the canonical. This continuity, visible over long periods of time and marked by changes that cumulatively transform the objects but are never so abrupt as

to break them, is called by various names: Tradition, Para-
dosis, Masorah. And since we are necessarily more involved
with the living than with the dead, with what learning cher-
ishes and interpretation refreshes rather than with mere remains, it seems necessary, even in this cursory glance at the
forces which direct and control the attention we pay to canonical objects, to say a word on Tradition.

The process of selecting the canon may be very long but,
once it is concluded, the inside works will normally be provided with the kinds of reading they require if they are to keep
their immediacy to any moment; that is, to maintain their
modernity. They quickly acquire virtual immunity to textual
alteration, so the necessary changes must all be interpretative;
and all interpretation is governed by prejudice. Consequently,
the need to remain modern imposes upon the chosen works
transformations as great as any they may have undergone in
precanonical redactions. They are inexhaustibly full of senses
only partly available to any previous reading, and the cumulative influence of tradition upon new readings is fitful and
partial. Every verse is occultly linked, in ways to be re-
searched, with all the others; the text is a world system. And
since the canonical work is fixed in time but applicable to all
time, it has figural qualities not to be detected, save at an
appropriate moment in the future. Interpretations may be regarded not as modern increments but rather as discoveries of
original meanings hitherto hidden; so that, together with the
written text, these interpretations constitute a total object of
which the text is but a part or version: an Oral Torah, or Oral
Tradition, preserved by an apostolic institution, equal in authority to and coeval with the written. This is the way in which
a transgenerational conversation plays the part of virtue
against fortune. Halakhic midrash extends and protects an
original body of law that would otherwise be in danger of
seeming obsolete and irrelevant, by subtle application to new
conditions. Haggadic midrash combines exegesis with new,
accommodating narratives. They assume an arche-Torah,
constituted by the text and all that is inexhaustibly said of it.

The purpose is to demonstrate that Torah is always completely significant. Those endless chains and crossings of significance, those condensations and displacements to which the normative interpretation attends, are as many as may be found in the created world with which the book is coextensive. The myth that sustains this interminable conversation of interpreters is, in short, that of the illimitable significance of a text-world, a world of truth to which opinion aspires.

That myth came into being when a cultus was destroyed; it took the place of a Temple, gave rise to a conversation which held together a nation and a religion through all vicissitudes. In practice it is a way of inferring the intention of a text from its exegetical products, which, in this sense, supersede the original text, doing the work that, before the canon existed, was done more simply by redaction. The flexibility of the method is augmented, rather than reduced, by the formation of hermeneutical rules, the *middot;* they facilitate free interpretation by use of analogy, parallelism, argument *a minori ad maius,* and so forth; it is a rhetorical repertoire that might well interest Paul de Man, perhaps especially in its handling of the requirement that the plain sense always be observed. For it has been shown that *peshat* really means authority; the plain sense is what the tradition, your teacher, says it is, and the semantics of the word show this.[6]

Out of this tradition, which developed orally over centuries, there came eventually a body of written interpretation which acquired authority second only to that of the sacred text, a commentary that was to sustain a metacommentary. And also out of the midrashic practice came much of the narrative of another sacred text, the New Testament, whose survival depended, at first, on its consonance with the parent canon, but which developed its own exclusiveness, and a relation partly antithetical to and partly complementary with that

6. See R. Loewe, "The 'Plain' Meaning of Scripture in Early Jewish Exegesis," in *Papers of the Institute of Jewish Studies London*, ed. J. G. Weiss (1964), 144–85.

ancestor, a relation of figural fulfillment. It too was to be regulated by an anterior oral tradition of which the new institution was the sole guardian, the sole judge between opinion (or heresy) and truth (or doctrine). Thus the community of interpretation persisted and proceeded with its purpose, divining the sense of the written text in accordance with interpretations posterior in promulgation but credited with oral priority, and so held to be matters of truth, not opinion.

These large instances of transgenerational consensus we may take as having, in their day, satisfied the need to disentangle knowledge from opinion, good doctrine from heresy. They could do so much less easily when the Tradition was challenged, as it was when the heresies of the Reformation challenged the institution that protected the Catholic tradition. The sacredness and integrity of the Scripture was not itself questioned, only its interpretative supplement; what had been truth was now condemned as erroneous opinion, as something that stood between the Christian and his text, preventing immediate access to it (for here was born another powerful myth).

In disowning the authority and the tradition, Reform showed how it is possible to alter the relation of center to margin. What mattered now were the words on the page. It was possible to attend closely to what had formerly been thought inconsiderable, and to dismiss as false any doctrinal interpretation which depended not on the Scripture but on the tradition, now disallowed on the ground that the original text, by virtue of its divine inspiration, was *sui ipsius interpres*. The belief that every man was his own priest and his own interpreter bred new heresies, including the heresy that only heretical interpretation can be valid. As in the history of Freudianism, wild interpretation contended with institutional dogma. New and less centrally powerful institutions could not prevent such developments, and (to compare great things with smaller) it can be said that the main effort of professional biblical scholarship since the Enlightenment has been to achieve for the Bible of Reform what Horne did for Botticelli, and Grierson for Donne: to bring to an object now revalued by opinion the benefits of accurate knowledge.

One effect of this development has been the dissolution of the canon into separate books, each with its own history, and it is fair to call this a remote consequence of the original attack on the institution. There is at this very moment an important argument in progress between scholars who wish to restore the virtues of canonicity, and those who think objective historical method the sole road to truth.[7] That truth is also likely to be imperfectly consistent with the assumption that the biblical texts report things as they really happened, which is why modern New Testament critics are showing some interest in secular literary theory, and especially theory of fiction. It is even argued that the future of Christianity may depend upon a new understanding of fiction as a form of truth. Perhaps this is to be thought of as a new way of opposing virtue to fortune in the interests of preserving the valued object, enabling the canon to survive.

Canons, which negate the distinction between knowledge and opinion, which are instruments of survival built to be time-proof, not reason-proof, are of course deconstructible; if people think there should not be such things, they may very well find the means to destroy them. Their defense cannot any longer be undertaken by central institutional power; they cannot any longer be compulsory, though it is hard to see how the normal operation of learned institutions, including recruitment, can manage without them.

One of the reasons why theological canons are difficult to defend is that knowledge has seemed to destroy many of the reasons for their being as they are; another is that very rigidity that was formerly a powerful protection. In thinking about canonicity in the history of the arts and literature, we

7. See Brevard S. Childs, *Introduction to the Old Testament as Scripture* (1979) and James Barr, *Holy Scripture: Canon, Authority and Criticism* (1983), for strongly opposed views. Also John Barton, *Reading the Old Testament* (1984).

have at once to reflect that our canons have never been impermeable; that our defenses of them are always more provisional than a church's would be; that we therefore have the advantage of being able to preserve the modernity of our choices without surrendering the right to add to them, even to exclude members of them, not by means of difficult administrative procedures but simply by continuing a conversation. We may quarrel, but on the whole everybody knows what is being talked about, even when the tone and content of the remarks are surprising. That is to say, the work of preservation and defense is carried on by many voices cooperating, however unwillingly, to one end, and not by a central authority resisting its challengers.

Perhaps some theologians envy us this freedom of opinion, engendered in part by the certainty that the value conferred by it upon the objects under discussion will outlive it, and outlive, too, the next re-siting of the center. What we have to remember as a condition of this liberty of interpretation is that we enjoy no privileged view, that we proceed with our interpretations from no confidence that we are somehow definitively seeing matters in their right proportions and relations at last.

That may appear to some an unduly bland account of our enterprise, for of late we have been more quarrelsome than usual, and there are apparently irreconcilable differences between us. They are, indeed, deep and extensive; and I can speak now only of a single aspect of them as it presents itself in relation to what I have said of Horne and Warburg, scholars dedicated, but by very different means, to the elucidation and preservation of the same object. Their attitudes are so different that one may think of them as representing a polarity that is natural, or customary, in the modern study of the past. Horne, though very conscious of the force of contemporary opinion, seems to have been aware of no impediment to the achievement, impossible to his predecessors only because they were ignorant, of immediate access to Botticelli and the Florence of his day. Warburg, who could not but be interested in the hermeneutics of his contemporary Dilthey,[8] was always conscious of the long perspectives of history, of the mystery of recurrence, the divine detail reappearing amid the changing configurations of the times. Out of such consciousness came systematic theories of history—Usener's, Vignoli's, Springer's, Warburg's own, built of the others: old systems revised, their complications analyzed into new principles. It seems to go without saying that no existing system, no former expression of principle, can serve. If all systems are erroneous, why bother with them? One answer—suggested by the reaction of Ernst Cassirer to Warburg's library—[9] would be that their preparation may require just such a collection, a sort of memory theater for the culture, affording successors the means of seeing new things and thinking new thoughts about human history. Another, more abstract, might be that it is on the face of it good to investigate the character of one's own presuppositions, and on the face of it bad to suppose that one has none. The belief of the hermeneuticists—that all interpretation has to take account of its own historical limitations—in the end demands a systematic philosophy and history. The belief of the "objectivists"—an inadequate label, but here it will serve—is that those limitations, in so far as they exist, are abrogated by learning and intelligent interpretative action.

Hans-Georg Gadamer, controverting the "objectivist" hermeneutics of Emilio Betti, makes this observation: "You know immediately when you read a classic essay by Mommsen the only time when it could have been written. Even a master of historical method is not able to keep himself entirely free from the prejudices of the time. Is this a failing? And even if it were, I regard it as a necessary philosophical task to consider why this failure is always present when anything is

8. Sassi, 88 (see chap. 1, n. 42).
9. See chap. 1, n. 53.

achieved."[10] The implication is that absolutely no such work could ever be free of prejudice, and that if it were, it could not succeed. It did not surprise us that Horne as well as Warburg was touched by contemporary prejudice, though Warburg gave the matter more thought. From the systems of his great predecessors—evidently unsatisfactory—he would make his own, conscious that it answered needs peculiar to himself, conscious also that it must, like theirs, fail, but supposing, like Gadamer after him, that this kind of failure is necessary to success.

Systems have not always been understood in this provisional, tentative manner. Coleridge, this time acknowledging his source in Schelling, observes in the *Biographia Literaria* that Leibniz could imagine a philosophy that would "explain and collect the fragments of truth scattered through systems apparently the most incongruous." Truth, though widely diffused, is often masked or mutilated by error; but, says Coleridge, one might assemble a philosophy composed of truths disentangled from Scepticism, Platonism, Neo-Platonism, Stoicism, Cabbalism, Hermeticism, Aristotelianism, and "the mechanical solution of all particular phenomena according to Democritus and the recent philosophers" that would present them "united in one central perspective point"; from that point alone one might perceive those regularities "which from every other point of view must appear confused and distorted." All that prevents our ascertaining this point is "the spirit of sectarianism."[11]

This vision of error at last purged, leaving single systematic truth, is constituted in part of the residues of Coleridge's own procedures. The dream-system is changeless and immovable, for any alteration would destroy the one position from which the whole can be seen. That position belongs to supreme authority; it is the throne of a duke or a king in a

10. H. G. Gadamer, *Truth and Method* (1960); 1975 trans., 465.
11. S. T. Coleridge, *Biographia Literaria* (1817), chap. xii.

Palladian theater. The only escape would be Blake's, to make one's own system in order not to be the slave of another man's; though Blake's decision is of course really Coleridge's also, differently viewed. And however often such dreams recur, changes in time and place and the conflict of the generations are their fatal opponents. And now we are taught that if true a system must be incomplete, and if complete untrue; or that system-makers ought to build into their systems a recognition that they are bound to be erroneous, and destined to obsolescence or oblivion.

One of the factors ensuring the fallibility of system is the recognition that all observation is dependent upon theoretical presupposition; for such presupposition must vary from age to age, from one community of interpretation to another, and even from one individual to another. There are modern philosophies which hold that something of the sort is true even of the natural sciences—that scientific truth is theory-dependent. Granted, then, that theories are what anybody can have, scientific truth is also a matter of opinion. This "epistemological anarchism," most forcibly stated by Paul Feyerabend,[12] is echoed in other sorts of philosophy by thinkers who may be more reluctant to go so far, but who nevertheless reject "the given"; who "decry the very notion of having a view," though finding themselves in the awkward position of having to offer one. They know, as Richard Rorty puts it, that "this century's 'superstition' was the last century's 'triumph of reason,' " and they know their own work "loses point when the period they were reacting against was over."[13] They look at past systems, not for building materials, but in order to bulldoze a space where the conversation game can continue on its unpredictable course; a game in which we may acquire

12. Paul K. Feyerabend, *Philosophical Papers* (2 vols.) 1982; and a review of these books by David Papineau, *Times Literary Supplement*, 29 October 1982, 1198, from which the quotations are taken.

13. Richard Rorty, *Philosophy and the Mirror of Nature* (1980), 371, 369.

not knowledge but what Rorty calls "wonder," rather aptly echoing Bacon's definition of wonder as "broken knowledge."

In this mood or atmosphere it is impossible that the sort of system toward which Warburg labored can for long be of more than antiquarian interest; but the same has to be said of any other, for example of any that presupposes the possibility of access to the past "as it really was," to the truth as it really was for some remote author and his original audience. And simply as to "theory-ladenness," there is very little to choose between Warburg and Horne, or between modern "objectivist" and "historicist" hermeneutics or, for that matter, between the "epistemological anarchists" of modern literary criticism, such as Stanley Fish, and their conservative opponents. All one can do is repeat that Warburg and those like him are more conscious of the nature of their intellectual procedures, and of the fallibility which is inseparable from their usefulness. Believing that the relation of past to present, any present, is mysterious, which the other party does not, one is obliged to make rational conjectures about it, and to suppose that by taking account of its great complexity one can speak more usefully about it than if one merely ignored it. There is, in short, a powerful notion, perhaps one could even call it a myth, that somehow everything hangs together and that one can at least begin to show how. So Warburg seeks clues to the structure and operation of the *Nachleben* in Darwin on the animal origins of human facial expressions, in the history of magic, in Vignoli's philosophy of fear, in the mnemic engrams of Semon. He contemplates these mysteries—continuities and discontinuities of attention, the recurrences of images, of ideas; he studies memory but also forgetting, and repetitions conscious and unconscious; he sees that nothing is as simple as the objectivists suppose, whether in the cultural or the individual history.

Freud, his contemporary, was another system-builder, another tinkerer with his own and other systems, who also found in the prehistory of a symptom or of an image continuities and gaps which were repeated in transindividual history. He believed, also, that to have real explanatory power a theory must contend with everything. That everything somehow hangs together is therefore presupposed, though it is also presupposed that there is a great deal to explain. Warburg knew, perhaps more clearly than his greater contemporary, that the conditions under which they did their thinking were in part determined, that they had no absolute control over them. Time would lay its hand on their systems; but they might by then have done their work, and they might also have their own *Nachleben,* either as deposits in the thought of others or in the doctrines of an institution such as that of psychoanalysis, intensely schismatic yet still recognizing the authority of its original foundations. Of at least one more matter these two had comparable awareness, and that is the working of a certain fortuity in their systematic operations: the luck of the third ear or eye, the special grace of divination.

The recent history of such awareness may be sought among the ruins of the systems of Warburg's half-forgotten mentors. It is handsomely illustrated in Lionel Gossman's recent study of the relations of Bachofen and Mommsen as sponsors of competing views about antiquity.[14] Bachofen is now remembered (in the United States and Britain) only for his belief in a primitive epoch of matriarchy or "mother-right." This doctrine left its mark on the thought of Engels, Freud, and Jung, but is not now accepted. However, there was much more to Bachofen. He shared with Nietzsche, a fellow-citizen of Basel, the view that the ancient world as represented by the dominant nineteenth-century philologists was a sham, the product of their own odious and alien civilization. Bachofen's views were taken up by the circle of Stefan George, a *foyer* now almost universally reprehended. Gadamer indeed blames the scholar for fostering "modern ersatz-religions" and so allowing himself to be used—"the victim of the mono-

14. Lionel Gossman, *Orpheus Philologus: Bachofen versus Mommsen on the Study of Antiquity, Transactions of the American Philosophical Society,* vol. 73, part 5 (1983).

mania of his own intuitions"—by precursors of Nazism.[15] Gossman remarks that such criticism, though not wholly unjust, is certainly insufficient, for it ignores Bachofen's criticism of the culture that supported the assurance of such historians as Mommsen; and it also ignores his altogether more profound understanding of the relations of past and present.

Bachofen's motto, *antiquam exquirite matrem,* would suit many historians, but it had a special aptness in his case. He also liked to compare the historian's task with that of Oedipus unravelling fatal enigmas, and that of Orpheus, bridging the worlds of living and dead.[16] For such work empirical knowledge was of course as necessary to him as to Warburg, and also to more "objective" historians, including those who may think they need very little else. But Bachofen believed the past could not be known were there not, between it and the present, a mode of correspondence which has its habitation deep in the human mind; so that he could speak, as Warburg might have done, of an ancient burial sculpture as being recognized only by virtue of that occult correspondence.[17] It seems fitting that between his scholarship and his personal life there is a concinnity not unlike that which Warburg discovered in himself. His antiquity was a compensation for his having to live in a world so distasteful, a world suffering from a malaise of which positivist "scientific" philology was a sign or symptom. His contact with the past was not, like that of Mommsen, unproblematical; it was rather a recognition of the sort that Warburg experienced when, into the Flemish bourgeois costumes of fifteenth-century Florence, or into a later modern world of telegrams and art nouveau, there erupts the ancient figure of the maenad.

For good or ill, it was the fate of both Bachofen and Warburg to become parts of a living tradition, to survive, transformed, into an unpredictable but not discontinuous future. Gadamer notices that Mommsen, so far from transcending his

15. Gadamer, 462. 16. Gossman, 38. 17. Gossman, 49.

epoch, is very distinctly identified with it. Nietzsche, who in his own way had some sympathy with much of Bachofen's thinking, scorned what he called "the increasing demand for historical judgment," taking it to be a form of apocalypticism, "as if our time were the latest possible time, an old age of the world in which it is timely to cast up our accounts." The validity of this comment is clear whenever one reads critics who assume that their precursors were limited by their historical situation, all the while assuming that they themselves are not. The Nietzschean position is more intelligent, for it is not intelligent to ignore the abundant evidence of the failure of apocalypticism, or to be the unconscious servant of such a myth. It is also more modest, for it avoids the boast that one's vantage point is uniquely privileged; and lastly it is more vivifying, for instead of trying to close history at the point where one stands, it looks to a future in which perhaps you yourself, certainly your descendants, will be working. *Memento vivere,* says Nietzsche;[18] remember too that you will become a small part of a living tradition of interpretation, part of the dialectic between opinion and knowledge.

That none of this is new doctrine the mention of Nietzsche will remind us. *Memento vivere* includes *memento mori;* though death may be mitigated by some small measure of survival and recurrence in the tradition, you will not expect to be treated as if you had been *dans le vrai.* Your systems will be read as fictions, which is indeed what they are in the Nietzschean view; for if the mind is an instrument for arranging the world in accordance with its own needs and desires, its arrangements must be fictive. In my first lecture, I mentioned E. H. Gombrich's question as to whether Warburg's symbols were meant to be real or only metaphors. For Nietzsche, the question would lack force; he would presumably have thought that

---

18. F. Nietzsche, *The Use and Abuse of History* (1873); 1949 trans. Nietzsche says of the relation of classical scholars to the Greeks: "They have nothing to do with each other, and this is called 'objectivity'!"

Warburg's symbols served him as did those of Yeats in his system: they are ways of holding together justice and reality in a single thought, where justice is a manner of thinking about the world that is congenial to the thinker, and likely to sustain his project when reality of itself is not. Or: such metaphors are ways of redescribing the world according to a new model. The model will become obsolete. To see in the course of the continuing conversation that it is so, why it is so, and what were the benefits of its not, in its time, having been so, may afford one instance of disentangling knowledge from opinion, except that the process of doing so will itself be subjected to the same discipline. Deconstructive thinkers know this well, but it is difficult to act upon the knowledge; for to know it is to know something of what it means to know, and so we arrive at that characteristic moment of deconstructive thinking, the aporia. Even Richard Rorty has a tendency, having shattered system, to assume that we can, by our own critique, get things right and keep them so in a sort of philosophical *nunc stans*. In his concluding remarks he says that he does not know what elsewhere he shows many signs of knowing—namely whether we are now at the end of an era; a hesitation this, a standing back from apocalypse. And I think of Wallace Stevens's contribution to this conversation, expressed in an aphorism, which should please Rorty: "The imagination is always at the end of an era." It is the profoundest of the Adagia.

Stevens further observed that the probings of the philosopher are deliberate, but the probings of the poet fortuitous; which gives another reason why it is so hard to make lasting matches between poetry and systematic thought. But I have argued that although they are mortal, and even in their day less powerful than more or less ignorant opinion, such systems serve as preservatives and stimulants; aphorisms and *obiter dicta* (*pace* Rorty) can hardly do the work, if only because the togetherness of the world, the idea of order mischievously or accidentally obscured, is a fiction that haunts us like Coleridge's fantasy of an unalterable ordered perspective.

I have been using Johnson's formulaic distinction between knowledge and opinion as a *point de retour,* but by this time it is clear, I suppose, that it will not serve, the distinction being archaic and without much application to the present state of things. There is a conversation, and in its course it has veered very far away from such certainties; one man's nature is another man's custom and, indeed, it is hard now to think of nature or of knowledge as having the degree of definition necessary to the construction of a Johnsonian sentence, distinguishing them with such antithetical force from their opposites. If they are to take any part in the conversation they must be reduced to conversational counters, they must be capable of being used in a game of which the chief characteristic is the discard.

That the conversation, the game, must go on, I have no doubt at all, for it is the means by which the primary objects of my own attention have to be brought to the attention of another generation. Thrilling new turns in the talk are the prerogative, no doubt, of the young. Dryden observed that old men should not

> . . . from the dregs of life hope to receive
> What the first sprightly running could not give—

and these lines were quoted by David Hume and later by Nietzsche.[19] It is not to be expected that future conversational developments will satisfy when the old ones have proved unsatisfying. In the past generation or so systems and theories of criticism have followed one another with exceptional rapidity, have sunk into history as missing what has come to seem to be the nature of the case. As a historian of sorts, I have always been interested in them without ever wanting to fight under their banners, seeing them rather as the transient agents of an extremely complex tradition. But I agree with

19. My friend John Wain, joining the succession, called his youthful autobiography *Sprightly Running;* I hope the sequel is not to be entitled *The Dregs of Life.*

those who say that the idea of tradition has never been so weak as it now is, the sense of a literary past less strong; and I therefore respect, in the work of such writers as Gadamer and Jauss, the attempt to make historical consciousness a modern and acceptable idea.

If this sounds too gloomily resigned, let me add that canonicity still seems to me an important preservative and, though under repeated attack, still potent. Opinion still has some power to maintain canons. A trivial instance: I recently introduced into a graduate class which was accustomed to dealing with higher things Arnold Bennett's novel *Riceyman Steps*, which I admire. It happens to be an almost exact contemporary of *Ulysses*. The first reaction of this extremely intelligent group was to ask what this text was doing in this class. It happens that right in the middle of the novel, and of obvious structural importance, there is a wedding cake.[20] Reaching for the tool of comparison, a very good student placed this wedding cake beside the one in *Madame Bovary*. That was enough; he felt no need of the other tool, that of analysis, for Bennett's cake crumbled to nothing in the presence of the august canonical cake of Flaubert. In the general discussion, such value as was conceded to Bennett's book was almost entirely historical; it gave some representation of the lives of the London poor and the lower middle classes in the years immediately after the First World War; it exploited with skill the now dead English novelistic tradition of facetiousness, and so on. It was never for a moment given the sort of consideration, the form of attention, reserved for books deemed to belong to what was frequently named "the modernist canon."

For books held to belong to that canon are granted not only high value but an almost rabbinical minuteness of comment and speculation. People of my age, which is after all not prodigious, can easily remember a time when *Ulysses* was not

20. For more about the wedding cake, see Kermode, *The Art of Telling* (1983), Prologue.

so favored; yet now it is seemingly secure, whereas *Riceyman Steps* is merely apocryphal, and likely to fade away. *Ulysses*, that is, has acquired perpetual modernity, guaranteed by continuous and fertile interpretation, but *Riceyman Steps* sinks into history—at best, fodder for Marxist analyses.

To be inside the canon is to be protected from wear and tear, to be credited with indefinitely large numbers of possible internal relations and secrets, to be treated as a heterocosm, a miniature Torah. It is to acquire magical and occult properties that are in fact very ancient. Sir Thomas Browne described the world as a "universal and public manuscript,"[21] a conceited account of Augustine's notion of the world as a poem, visible and accessible to all, though its correspondences are closed to all but the most penetrating minds. Baudelaire gave the idea a powerful modern formulation in a famous sonnet. The equation goes two ways: if the world is a book, gathered, when rightly seen, into one volume, then the book is a world, capable of being exfoliated into a universe. All discords can be resolved into concords, whether in the heavens or on the page. For the book or the world time stops; only the observers, the interpreters, are mutable and subject to temporal attrition.

These interpreters are required to be vigilant and industrious, for to maintain a canonical work, to keep it in a condition of timeless modernity, is a never-ending and delicate business. That is why the canon, though not closed, is hard to get into. Applicants are often advised to apply to some other canon, say the "postmodern" one. The struggle for admission to the "modernist canon" could be illustrated from the case of Ford Madox Ford's *The Good Soldier*, which is still in the waiting room, or even on the threshold. More fortunate for once, Conrad was long ago admitted, though his presence demands at least as much of the interpreters. In fact, it is not difficult to imagine the kind of commentary that would sustain

21. *Religio Medici* (1643), I.16.

the modernity of Ford's novel. Its anachronies could be given, if the novel had the status of heterocosm, a quasi-theological status; they would be aspects of a world like God's, in which, as Boethius tells us, the human sense of serial order is only an illusion. God's world is like a Fordian "affair," in which sequence is reduced as far as may be to simultaneity, a *nunc stans;* a world in which trivial events and encounters have great figural power. But of course there is no limit to the variety of ways in which, once admitted, it might be endorsed and confirmed in its position; there could not be, since if all interpretation save a remnant passed on as tradition is, unlike its subject, mortal, there must in principle always be the possibility of fresh supplies.

When Paul de Man remarks that a canon has its status from the value of its constituents, I have to demur; the truth must, at least in part, be the other way round. But when he says that interpretation is only the possibility of error, and that it is not Rousseau but his interpreters who are blind, he is more convincing, for what he says of Rousseau is what it is necessary to think of all canonical books, and the blindness of interpreters is a necessary condition of that thought. De Man gives *Blindness and Insight* a marvelous epigraph from Proust: "Cette perpetualle erreur, qui est précisément la vie . . ."[22] The blindness is vital and beneficent, for all interpretations are erroneous, but some, in relation to their ultimate purpose, are good nevertheless, saying what they had not meant or more than they meant, and defeating time. Perhaps a perfect interpretation would, as Valéry said of pure reality, stop the heart. Good enough interpretation is what encourages or enables certain necessary forms of attention.

What matters, so far as I can see, is that ways of inducing such forms of attention should continue to exist, even if they are all, in the end, dependent on opinion. The mere possibility that something of value will not fall under the rule of time—

22. Paul de Man, *Blindness and Insight* (1971).

and here we need not raise the question of how that value originated, whether inherent or the creation of interpreters— is the real justification for our continuing the clamorous, opinionated conversation.

Since I believe this, it will be clear that I have failed to distinguish knowledge from opinion, or even that which is established because it is right from that which is right only because it is established. Simply: whatever takes the part of virtue against fortune, whatever preserves and restores some object of which the value may have been or may be in danger of getting lost is, however prone to error, good. So Warburg's phobic engrams are good, and so are the allegorizations of the Song of Songs and the now institutionalized "readings" of *Ulysses*, and the myths of heterocosm or the dissociation of sensibility. Also, the arguments against all these things can be good. What is not good is anything whatever that might destroy the objects valued or their value, or divert from them the special forms of attention they have been accorded.

These meditations, for they are hardly arguments, arise from my remarks in the first two lectures. Opinion, with the smallest admixture of anything that might by courtesy be called knowledge, restored to our attention Botticelli, as it restored Donne. So restored, the paintings and the poems looked different, but looked modern and immediate to us, like a verse from the Law as expounded by a sage. The confirmation of Botticelli in what came to seem his proper place was effected by speculation sometimes systematic and therefore prone to rapid obsolescence, and sometimes conspicuous for its attempt to avoid system or theory, though some form of theory seems necessary to all forms of attention.

Later I exercised myself in an attempt to marginalize what had been the central interest of many generations of *Hamlet*, and to put in the central position an aspect of the play that had been regarded as merely peripheral. This kind of thing— often done, often deplored—will always remain to do again.

The work easily tolerates such treatment, as it must if it is to be preserved, and preserved not in an archive but in the modern mind. As a matter of fact there was a considerable quantity of evidence, yielding itself easily to this altered perspective, which I refrained from using. But there is a canon of interpretation which I have only now formulated and perhaps should have produced and observed earlier, to the effect that in the ordinary way one ought not to bore one's listeners, one's partners in the conversation; and it was this consideration that prevented me from piling it on.

All such centralities (or centralizations) are in the nature of the case precarious. Anybody can remarginalize what I have centralized and centralize something else; anybody (to borrow a fashionable and sprightly running terminology) can re-hierarchize the elements I was at pains to de-hierarchize. Now I am trying to behave as others, above commended, have behaved, to resist the illusion that what I am saying can have any permanent rightness or value. It may still be asked why, in that case, I have gone to some trouble to say it. The best answer to that question is one I find in the writing of D. C. Hoy: "We hold our present beliefs because we think they are supported and supportable. We recognize, however, that if new evidence to the contrary arises, we would be willing and likely to change our beliefs. Until that time, there is no reason for not believing what we believe. The belief that beliefs change does not therefore mean that no belief is possible any longer."[23] As Hector rather inconsequently remarks in Shakespeare's *Troilus and Cressida,* this is my "opinion in way of truth," and I think it is something like the truth about the opinion many of us hold, at the present moment, as to the necessity of carrying on doing things with—and for—literature.

23. D. C. Hoy, *The Critical Circle* (1978); 1980 ed., 139.